top·o·nym·i·ty

top·o·nym·i·ty

AN ATLAS OF WORDS

John Bemelmans Marciano

BLOOMSBURY

NEW YORK   BERLIN   LONDON   SYDNEY

Published by Bloomsbury USA, New York

All papers used by Bloomsbury USA are natural, recyclable products made
from wood grown in well-managed forests. The manufacturing processes
conform to the environmental regulations of the country of origin.

LIBRARY OF CONGRESS CATALOGING-IN-PUBLICATION DATA

Marciano, John Bemelmans.
Toponymity : an atlas of words / John Bemelmans Marciano.—1st U.S. ed.
    p. cm.
Includes bibliographical references and index.
ISBN-13: 978-1-60819-370-7 (alk. paper)
ISBN-10: 1-60819-370-5 (alk. paper)
1. English language—Etymology. I. Title.
PE1580.M37 2010
422.03—dc22

                              2010030616

First U.S. Edition 2010

10   9   8   7   6   5   4   3   2   1

Printed in the U.S.A. by Quad/Graphics, Fairfield, Pennsylvania

For Andromache

INTRODUCTION

Imagine you are an intrepid young Cro-Magnon who, like so many Cro-Magnons before you, has found a lovely spot in Europe in which to settle, only to find it occupied by a motley tribe of stocky, red-haired Neanderthals. Might making right, you kick them out, but as they are packing up their gear, you see them pointing over in the direction of a tall mountain and saying "Schtroumpf" (or that's what it sounds like anyway). So you and your people start calling it Mount Schtroumpf, and the river that flows from there the River Schtroumpf, and the berries growing on its slopes schtroumpfberries. In fact, the berries are so delicious that you sell them to the Cro-Magnons in the next valley over, who simply call them schtroumpfs, or rather strumbs, because they don't understand your language any better than you do theirs.

Future Cro-Magnon etymologists may consider the origin of *strumb* to be the name of a mountain, or they may even realize it is a Neanderthal word, but they won't get any further than that. Truth is, we can never get to the ultimate origin of any word. But is it not different for place names? Is there not something more elemental about them?

We tend to have this idea that names are not words—they aren't in dictionaries, right?—but that isn't true. Names are words for specific things, while words are the names of something general. In English, we have the funny custom of capitalizing the former and lowercasing the latter, making a minor distinction seem great. The Morgue was the name of a building in Paris where they kept the dead; *morgue* is the word for that kind of building anywhere. Names and words operate under the same rules; they shift meaning from one thing to the next, from schtroumpf to Mount Schtroumpf to strumb, and what was once a word becomes a name and back again.

For a specific example, take Atlas, pictured on the cover of this book. If I ask you for a road atlas, does an image of him pop into your head? Or the title of a far-too-long Ayn Rand novel? Or the Atlantic Ocean? As a word, name, or title, all atlases come back to that Titan shouldering his burden. His name, in turn, is thought to come from a word that meant "the bearer," but was he even the first to be called that? In ancient Greek cosmology, Mount

2

Atlas itself was believed to hold up the sky (*something* obviously had to), so quite possibly the title of bearer went to the mountain, and the legend that was applied to it—of a defeated god's punishment—came later.

As for *schtroumpf*, it probably wasn't a Neanderthal toponym at all; more likely it was simply their word for mountain, or maybe what the mountain reminded them of (as Grand Teton is rumored to be French for Giant Ta-ta). Or, if the experience of American names adopted from native languages is to be our guide, it had absolutely nothing to do with that mountain at all.

(For what the word *schtroumpf* really means, by the way, see p. 121.)

A surprising thing happened on the way to making this book, which aimed to be part dictionary, part atlas, and part encyclopedia: It took on a narrative. A jumbled, hypertextual sort of narrative, to be sure—the nature of an alphabetical list of entries ensures that—but one with constantly intertwining characters and stories just the same.

The central theme of this book is exchange, its plot twist the advent of the Age of Exploration, when the trading of goods and ideas from different worlds began to take place across oceans rather than along seacoasts and riverbanks and through wastelands. Along the way, we have story after story that describes the experience of meeting the *other*. The English language helps us excavate this history, revealing its own perceptions plus the ones of all the languages from which it has adopted vocabulary. French, Spanish, Latin, Greek, Arabic: In the etymological fossil record of them all are the perceptions and prejudices of peoples who considered themselves Us and everyone else Them. Toponymous words provide a story of the best and worst of human interaction; some of them document our innate human curiosity about a world beyond our own, while others betray our xenophobia.

So how do place names become words? Most often, they are added to the name of a product. The idea of a far-away place where something grows or is made the best has a powerful pull; the added cost of getting it from there to here only adds to its mystique.

This is a phenomenon as old as the marketplace, or souk. In the *Arabian Nights*, there is a tale of a porter of Baghdad who is hired by a mysterious woman; the porter understands her to be wealthy from the Mosul cloak the lady wears, and from what she buys: Hebron peaches, Turkish quinces, Nile cucumbers, Egyptian limes, Aleppo jasmine, Damascus peaches, Aleppo raisins, Iraqi sugarcane, Ba'albak figs, candles of Alexandria wax, and hard Syrian cheese. How far we are willing to go and at what cost we are willing to get something is a calculation we make every day, whether we shop at the corner store, Whole Foods, or Walmart.

Once a mark of quality is set, however, there is only one way to go: down. Thus, the good name of Italian Parmigiano cheese has become the horror of supermarket Parmesan. (How long has that shaker been sitting on the pizzeria counter, exactly?) At best, the ubiquity of a given product turns its name into something generic—i.e., cologne. At worst, it is used so aggressively that it falls victim to what's been called the euphemism treadmill or carousel: how *coach* went from being what only the nobility rode in to the most uncomfortable, degrading traveling compartment in the world.

Another common way for a name to become a word is by comparison. We use this all the time: *Stop acting like a barbarian/a middle schooler/a baby.* In this way, the name of a people enters the general lexicon. A gay woman is called a lesbian because of a famed Lesbian poet. As Lesbos is an island, *lesbian* is a toponym.

But what of the phrase "to go dutch"—is that toponymous? The Dutch have two names for their country but are called after neither. Can you separate a place name from the people who live there? The answer is no.

The relationship of people and places over a given time period is at the very crux of toponymity. Names are ownership, and ownership is temporary; just ask the cheesemakers of Parma. Or the Greeks: The toponymy of Asia Minor has yielded more words than just about anywhere, and yet most of the old Hellenic place names have been scrubbed clean by the Turks, who brought names of their own. (Good luck trying to find Magnesia-on-the-Maeander on Google Maps.) Nor does it have only to do with one ethnicity replacing the other; within a given nation, a toponym can be an important political question. Burma or Myanmar?

To include words that come from peoples with names different from their homelands (or without homelands, as with the Gypsies) stretches the meaning of toponym. But this book aims to be as inclusive as possible. To that end, it lists words that come from the names of buildings, such as Paris's Morgue or the Mausoleum of Halicarnassus. There are physical phenomena, like winds that blow in certain seasons and not others, such as the monsoon. And then there are words that come from the names of self-selecting groups of peoples—assassins, buggers—that stretch the criteria to the limit but are included in the interests of good reading.

So in the end, what is toponymity? It, like most names, is not a word in dictionaries. *Toponym,* however, is. The Oxford English Dictionary defines it as "a place-name; a name given to a person or thing marking its place of origin"; the suffix -*ity*, meanwhile, comes from Latin, where it expressed a state or condition. The dictionary makers add that when -*ity* is applied in modern formulations, it produces "playful or pedantic nonce words." At the end of this book, I hope that you will think of the nonce word *toponym-ity* as expressing a playful and only occasionally pedantic look at the words that come from places and the peoples who live in them.

AUTHOR'S NOTE

The maps in this book are meant to illustrate the text and so present archaic and modern toponyms side by side. Note that not all names appearing on maps are entries, nor is it obvious from the text where the map for a given top-onym is located (if it is on a map at all).

EGYPT

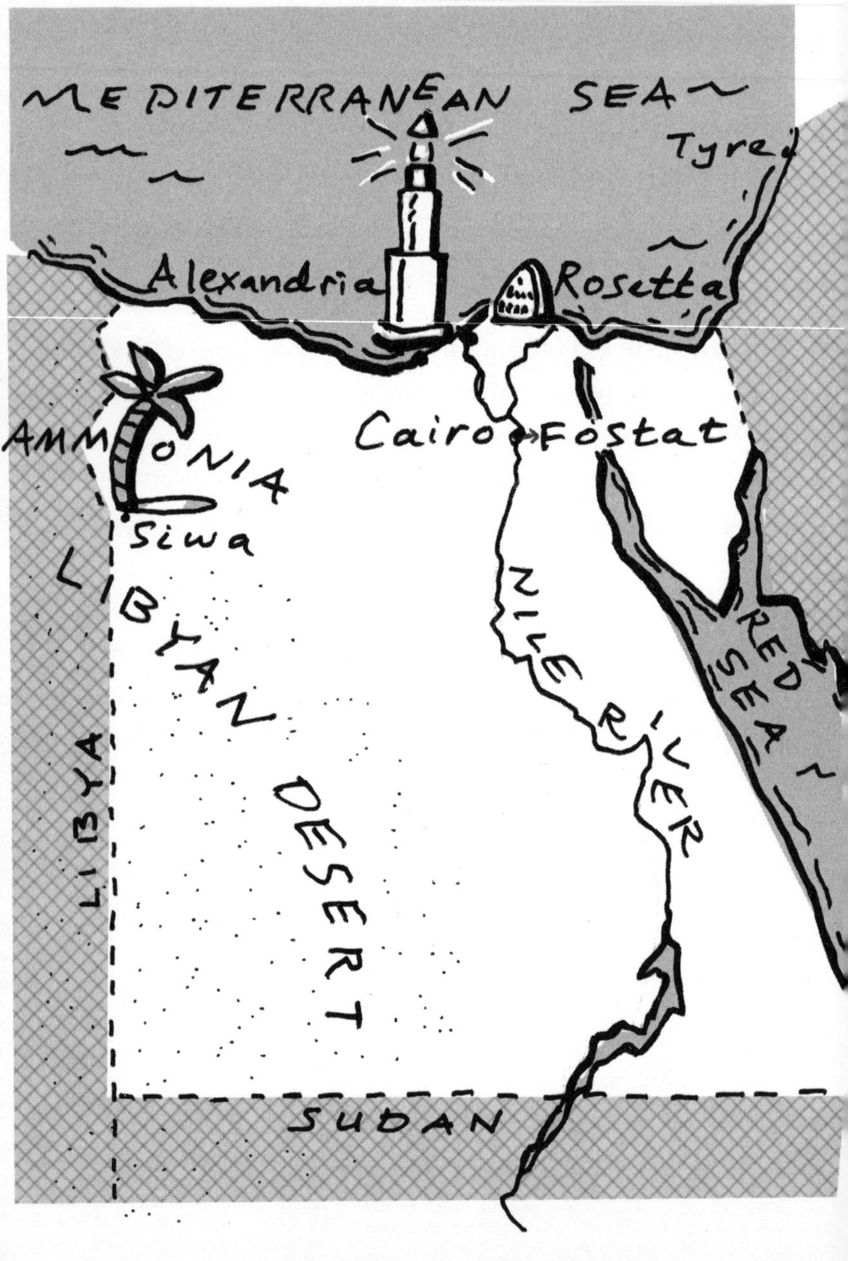
MEDITERRANEAN SEA
Tyre
Alexandria
Rosetta
Cairo
Fostat
AMMONIA
Siwa
LIBYAN DESERT
NILE RIVER
RED SEA
LIBYA
SUDAN

am·mo·nia *n. A gas of eye-watering pungency; familiar in its natural state to anyone who's ever cleaned out a stable or wandered down Bourbon Street at six in the morning.*

The oasis of Siwa lies in the remote Libyan Desert. The desert here is pure sand dunes, but the oasis is not the stereotypical two palm trees and a puddle of water; rather, it is a vast plantation of palm trees on the edge of a large saltwater lake. Siwa's most miraculous feature is its freshwater spring, called the Fountain of the Sun by the ancients because its waters ran cold at noon and boiled at midnight. The oasis was long considered a sacred site, with the Egyptians having built upon it a temple to the god Ammon. (He's the guy with the ram's head in the friezes.) Ammon intervened in human affairs through oracles, telling one visitor, Alexander the Great, that he was destined to be pharaoh. (Remarkably, this was just what the Macedonian wanted to hear.)

In reference to its temple, the oasis and its surrounding region were known as Ammonia. The Romans used Ammonia as a place of exile, and to mine a very particular kind of substance. Centuries of camel caravans stopping to refresh and relieve themselves had created enormous cesspool deposits of camel piss and manure, which the Romans are said to have harvested and used in the preparation of a crystal they called *sal ammoniacus* — the salt of Ammon. Many years later (in 1782, to be exact), the gas produced from ammoniac salt would be named after the region itself. See *attic* for another kind of salt, and *dollar* for other kinds of mines.

Ar·ma·ged·don *n. The battle to end all battles. For Christians, literally; for everybody else, figuratively.*

Thomas Jefferson remembered it as "the ravings of a maniac no more worthy nor capable of explanation than the incoherences of our own nightly dreams"; to many evangelical Christians, however, it is a roadmap of a future that can't come quickly enough. The Book of Revelation, aka the Apocalypse of John, has long been the most controversial book of the New Testament. Here's a taste:

> *16:13 And I saw three unclean spirits like frogs come out of the mouth of the dragon, and out of the mouth of the beast, and out of the mouth of the false prophet.*
> *16:14 For they are the spirits of devils, working miracles, which go forth unto the kings of the earth and of the whole world, to gather them to the battle of that great day of God Almighty.*

16:15 Behold, I come as a thief. Blessed is he that watcheth, and keepeth his garments, lest he walk naked, and they see his shame.

16:16 And he gathered them together into a place called in the Hebrew tongue Armageddon.

Although thought of as a spiritual conflict, the battle of Armageddon was named, like so many battles, for the locality in which it would—or will—take place. Revelation was written not by the baptizing John who lost his head, but another guy named John from the isle of Patmos. The book reads like an overheated graphic novel and was considered unworthy trash by many early church fathers. That said, it is awfully entertaining and makes for a slam-bang ending to the Bible. The Apocalypse was composed, like the rest of the New Testament, in Greek; the title is from *apokalyptein*, meaning "uncover," while *Armageddon* is a Hellenized rendering of *Har-Megiddon*, Hebrew for Mount of Megiddo, the site of many major battles that have already happened, some as far back as four thousand years ago. For such a major historical site, not to mention the future location of the ultimate earthly battle between good and evil, Megiddo today is a pretty sleepy Israeli town just down the way from Nazareth. It's got a kibbutz nearby, plus a regional airport, so when the forces of good and evil arrive, they will at least have a place to land.

See *bible* for more about the good book's Greekness.

as·sas·sin *n. A political murderer.*

"You shall learn all about the Old Man of the Mountain as I Marco heard related by many persons," began the Venetian traveler Marco Polo in his account of the Assassins, a Muslim sect that his audience was already well familiar with. The Old Man of the Mountain (OMM) was the European name for the Assassins' leader, a guy who comes off as a kind of medieval James Bond villain in Polo's rendering. In the garden of OMM's mountain-valley stronghold, he re-created Paradise as described by Muhammad, complete with fantastical animals, sexy singing women, and streams channeling fresh water, wine, honey, and milk. OMM would bring young men to his castle, slip them a mickey, and bring them into his tantalizing garden for a quick visit. Then he'd slip them another mickey, and they'd wake up with a taste for Paradise and a desire to do whatever it took to gain entry. (Much as for fundamentalist Christians, the end couldn't come fast enough.) OMM would then give them a killing assignment that would assure them of martyrdom if they happened to die in the act.

Polo's tale of the cult is one among many. The Assassins entered Western mind space during the Crusades, especially after a rumor circulated that Richard the Lionheart had hired a team of them to murder the French king Philip Augustus. The lyrics of Provençal troubadours further spread their reputation for terror. The Assassins were

ASIA MINOR

Soli

CILICIA

Antioch

Syrian Desert

Cyprus

Assassins

copper mines

papyrus

Byblos

Phoenicia

sea snails

Tyre

Damask (Damascus)

good vs. evil

Nazareth

Magdala

pillar of salt

Armageddon

Ascalon

Gaza

Philistia

Sodom

Gomorrah

the Levant

the sworn enemies of the respected Saracen warrior Saladin, who was said to have awoken one night in his heavily guarded tent to find a poisoned dagger, the signature warning of the Assassins. Its message: Withdraw from his fight against them or face the consequences. (He withdrew.) The Assassins were believed to gather courage for their nefarious deeds by getting high; in fact, *assassin* has long been believed to be a mangling of the Arabic term *hashishiyyin*, meaning "user of hashish."

Separating fact from fiction is all but impossible. What is known is that the Assassins were a messianic Shiite cult who controlled a major chunk of Syria and Persia beginning in the eleventh century and made effective use of political murder. The mythology surrounding them is said to be just another example of Western Orientalist fantasizing, especially the whole hashish idea. However, the source may not be the West but the Sunni Muslim Syrians who hated the Shiite Assassins; even if tales of their dope use are apocryphal—hashish isn't *usually* known for making a person want to go out and kill—to call the Assassins a bunch of worthless druggies would have been an effective means of dismissing and discrediting a despised enemy.

The extermination of the Assassins themselves was effected by Marco Polo's pals the Mongols, who broke them in 1256.

at·tic *n. The place where you put stuff you never want to see again, but can't bear to throw away.*

The most famous rivals among the ancient Greek city-states were Athens and Sparta, also known as Attica and Laconia after their respective hinterlands. Beyond being enemies, Athenians and Spartans were polar opposites. The Laconian mind-set is best revealed in the tale of the Spartan boy who went to school with a fox hidden under his shirt. While the teacher lectured, the fox gnawed and clawed at the child's innards; the boy didn't utter a peep, lest he be shamed, and fell dead to the floor, showing the sort of will and endurance that has led *spartan* to its proverbial use.

Athenians, on the other hand, were a much talkier sort; the phrase *Attic salt* (after the Latin *sal Atticum*) refers to a sharp but refined wit. Rather than in battle, the men of Athens made their most enduring marks in the fields of philosophy and architecture. On a classical façade, the Attic order of columns (generally pilasters) sits atop the much taller main order (whose columns may be freestanding). The area found behind this truncated order was called the Attic story, which is how the room at the top of your house that you have to bend over to move around in got its name.

For more on the famously tight-lipped Spartans, see *laconic*; for the loquacious Athenians, *stoic*.

bar·bar·i·an *n. A person of a race other than your own.*

The word *barbarian* has over the years functioned as an Us-vs.-Them club. This club was started by the Greeks, who considered everyone who wasn't Greek and didn't speak it to be *barbaros*. The Romans co-opted the term, as they did so much else Greek, and decided that they were a part of the club, too, but that everyone else *but* them and the Greeks lived in "Barbaria." As the empire expanded, Barbaria shrank, but that tide reversed course when the barbarians came a-sacking. As the Romans had done with the Greeks, these invaders adopted much of the culture of the conquered, including the Christian faith, and decided that the club was now religious and that the land of the infidel was Barbary. If you guess that this is how the Barbary Coast of North Africa got its name, though, you'd be wrong.

Barbara is not only the name of my mother, but Arabic for "to talk noisily or confusedly," and assumedly it's from this word (and not a borrowing of the Greek) that the terms *Barbary* and *Berber* arose: for the people and culture native to the area. (The Arabs, of course, have their own club, which the conquered Berbers were definitely not a part of.) While it seems like an awfully big coincidence, it isn't. Both words are likely onomato-poeic—imitative—in that when foreigners spoke, both Arabs and Greeks heard nothing but *barbarbarbar*.

For sacking barbarians, see *frank* and *lumber*; for people who could speak Greek but did it badly, *solecism*.

bay·o·net *n. Because sometimes a rifle isn't enough.*
A weapon said originally to be favored by Basque hunters in Bayonne. France, not New Jersey.

beg *v. To ask for something for nothing.*
Founded in the twelfth century in the Low Countries, the Beguines were a kind of independent order of female monks who went about helping the poor, old, and infirm. The Beguines had an almost hippie ethos, preferring to live outside of society, or at least the society around them, which wouldn't let women do much of anything. At first the Beguines were itinerant, but they went on to establish houses called Beguinages that they helped support by working as weavers; this was easy work to get in a country thick with looms, but weaving was looked down upon as a profession for women because of its imagined connection to black magic. (*Women weaving, they must be weaving spells*: Such was the medieval mind.) Because of all this, and because they refused to take vows that would have placed them within the Catholic power structure, they were looked upon with suspicion, and their name became synonymous with *heretic*. (Europe was thick with heretics at the time, so churchfolk were touchy.)

As happens to groups of single women, the Beguines began attracting guys. Men being then what they are now, many of them had far from charitable intentions. Because

there were no official vows to take and no overarching orga-
nization, any dude who wanted to call himself a Beguin was
free to do so. Mostly, Beguins seem to have been vagrants
pleading for alms for the poor—themselves—and such was
their reputation that they began to be called the Beghards,
-*ard* being a sneeringly negative suffix (e.g., coward, drunk-
ard, and bastard). And so, even though the Beguines were
never a mendicant order, their very name came to mean the
act of pleading for money—*begging*—a word that obviously
needed inventing.

For the European heretic infestation, see *bugger*; for beg confusion,
bigot.

bi·ble *n. The authoritative book, on anything.*
The Phoenicians, before establishing the first far-flung seafaring empire of the Mediterranean, were famed for their
excellence as traders. Gebhal was their main city in the
early days—the eleventh century B.C.—and it was here that
the Phoenicians developed the world's first phonetic (*not*
a toponym) writing system, using symbols based on Egyptian hieroglyphs. This alphabet thing was soon adopted by
another great seagoing folk, the Greeks, who spread it even
further. But the Phoenicians didn't only provide them the
letters to write with; they provided the Greeks the material
to write them down on.

Gebhal, which the Greeks called Byblos, was the port through which the Greeks got their hands on another Egyptian product, papyrus, which they also called *byblos*. By synecdoche, the name for the material became the word for the finished product (like when you write a "paper" for school), and the diminutive term *biblion* came to mean "book," a sense seen in *bibliophile* and *bibliography* as well as in *the* book, the Bible. Though it narrated the actions of Levantine people who mostly spoke Aramaic, the New Testament was written in Koine Greek, the literary language of the eastern Roman Empire. The first copies were written on papyrus, a material that ages poorly, which is one reason why so few early editions have survived, and even then only in fragmentary form. The earliest good-quality copies of the Bible date to the fourth century, when scribes had switched to a more durable material.

The use of treated animal skins for writing had begun much earlier; in the second century B.C., it became popular when papyrus shortages in Alexandria ran up prices. Pergamon, the seat of a kingdom whose reach stretched across most of Asia Minor at one time, not only produced fine calfskin vellum but was a major consumer of it, having the second-largest library in the world after Alexandria. The Romans called this vellum *pergamena*, the source (albeit many times corrupted) of our English word *parchment*.

FRANCE
ENGLISH CHANNEL
Cambrai
Chantilly
JERSEY
Seine
Paris
NORMANDY
Vire
ATLANTIC OCEAN
MTNS
LIMOUSIN
Évian
Lascaux
Cro-Magnon
Albi
Nîmes
Marseille
Bayonne
THE MED
Seine
Châtelet
le Morgue
ÎLE de la CITÉ
la BOHÈME
LATIN QUARTER
PARIS

big·ot *n. A person of unshakable preconceived notions, all negative.*

Did *Beguine* beget *bigot?*

Not originally. In the twelfth century, the word *bigot* debuted as a slur Frenchmen applied to the Normans. The term *Norman* simply means "North-man," and referred to Scandinavians generally (*Norse* and *Norway* have similar roots). When they oared their longships up the Seine and besieged Paris in the late 800s, the Normans were decidedly Viking, but they liked what they saw and went native, which is to say they settled in Normandy and became French, or tried. Their adoption of French language, religion, and customs notwithstanding, they were unloved by the natives, snooty as ever.

King Charles the Simple created the duchy of Normandy to get the Normans to stop attacking France, and also to provide a line of defense from other Viking attackers. (Good thinking.) The legend goes that Rollo, the Norman leader, refused to kiss the foot of King Charles to show his ducal fealty, and uttered the oath *Bi got!* to emphasize it. This curse—By god!—was seriously blasphemous back in the day, but the tale rings untrue. The foot-kissing part, anyway. It's actually quite plausible that *Bi got!* is the origin of *bigot*, as the French have a history of calling foreigners by their favorite curses. During the Hundred Years War, English occupiers were *les goddons*—a French rendering of *goddamns*—and the American "liberators" of World War II *les somnobiches*.

Whatever the origin of the word, *bigot*'s sense changed from meaning a Norman to a religious hypocrite, from which we get our English term of intolerance. Interestingly, early on in English the word referred to female religious hypocrisy, which has led to the conjecture that bigots got confused with Beguines, those untrustworthy, do-goody weaving women.

For the Beguines, see *beg*; for a proud Norman, *vaudeville*.

~

LOATHE THY NEIGHBOR

Englishmen have pretty much considered anyone that they've ever come into contact with as being lazy, poor, cowardly, untrustworthy, thieving, and of substandard morality, a mind-set of superiority reflected in a litany of set phrases in the language. Particular proverbial scorn has been heaped upon those peoples the English share the island of Great Britain with: the Scottish and the Welsh.

Most of the terms deriding the Scottish have long since fallen into disuse. A Scotch prize is captured by mistake, a Scotch marriage is two people shacking up. The sole remaining term of mockery is Scotch tape, which supposedly got its name from being cheaply manufactured. The long history of pejorative terms using *Scotch*, however, made the word itself derogatory. It is now only okay to use *Scotch* if you're talking about whisky. As for the Welsh, their very name comes from an ancient Germanic term meaning "foreigner" (note the related *Walloon*, and *walnut*, which means "a foreign nut"), showing that they have always been aliens to the Anglos-Saxons. The old horse-racing term for not making good on a bet—*welshing*—is still in use, as is *Welsh rarebit*, originally *Welsh rabbit*, in reference to the people of Wales being so impoverished that their idea of meat was cheese on toast.

Surprisingly, those who got the worst of English abuse were the Dutch. Most expressions we now use concerning the people of Holland are harmless, such as *Dutch door*, *double Dutch*, and *Dutch oven*, but previously, terms containing *Dutch* were the idiomatic equivalent of a Polack joke. A bookie who loses money is a Dutch book; Dutch courage is inspired only by booze; if you're in Dutch, you're in prison, or pregnant; and a Dutch widow is a prostitute. Still in wide use is *to go Dutch*, which describes an action—not paying for your date—that languages around the rest of the globe call *to go American*.

More complicated have been English attitudes toward their eternal nemesis, the French. The English language shows admiration for Gallic high culture, as evidenced in fashion, with French cuffs, and especially in food, with

French getting positively applied to bread, toast, dressing, onion soup, and fries. On matters of sex, however, the English exhibit a mixture of envy and denigration when they look across the Channel. Syphilis is the French disease (or French pox, or French evil, or French compliment), a condom with protuberances is a French tickler, and to use *french* as a verb means to kiss with open mouths and tussling tongues.

America, with its shorter history and fewer neighbors, has not produced as many idioms of this type, and most of them have to do with the original peoples of the continent. Most prominently, there is *honest Injun* (as in, not very) and *Indian giver*. Many believe that our current usage of Indian giver is backward—that originally it was the white man reneging on land deals who was the Indian giver. Sadly, this is an urban legend: The phrase apparently dates to a particular tribe of Native Americans who, when gifting, expected a gift of similar value in return or wanted their own back. What made colonialists consider this a gift at all, however, shows the level of awareness and sensitivity with which the "settling" of America was undertaken.

For another Americanism of this sort, see *gyp*; for how Anglo-Saxons are not alone in their opinion of other cultures, *barbarian*.

bi·ki·ni *n. A two-piece swimsuit of immoderate proportions; the more immoderate, the better.*

The summer of 1946 brought two new things to the beach: one, atomic testing in the South Pacific; two, scandalously scanty swimwear.

With joyous liberation in the air and Europeans hitting the *plages* and *spiagge* for something other than military operations, a couple of French designers had it in their mind to produce a racier version of the two-piece bathing suit. First came Jacques Heim, who designed what he claimed to be the world's smallest swimsuit and dubbed it the Atom. Next was Louis Réard, an auto engineer who made his living running his mom's lingerie shop. Réard's swimsuit was *really* tiny—skimpier than most of the lingerie he sold. The crucial difference was that, while Heim's Atom, like its dowdier predecessors, kept the navel tucked away out of sight, in Réard's work the wearer's belly button was gloriously exposed.

Réard unveiled his creation in Paris on July 5, hiring a stripper to show it off, as no professional model was willing to appear so naked in public. Claiming to have "split the Atom," Réard proclaimed his swimsuit the bikini. American nuclear testing at Bikini Atoll had begun a few days earlier and captured the world's attention, and just in case anyone was missing the point of the sensation he wanted to create, Réard's two-piece suit was printed with images of newspaper type. Wishful thinking, wish fulfilled. As far as the sensation went, anyway; as for it becoming a popular fashion, the bikini was a dud. It took until the 1960s, when people began feeling liberated in a different way, for navels to be regularly and freely expressed in public.

Réard would go to his grave feeling cheated, having made no money off his creation; the Bikini Atollers, on the other hand, were paid a fortune but it gave them little solace. The U.S. government had asked the Atollers, for the good of mankind, to take a little vacation while the military ran some important experiments on their land. The Atollers, who numbered fewer than two hundred, got shuttled around the Marshalls while their islands got nuked into a radioactive wasteland; those islands, that is, that weren't vaporized entirely during America's one and only hydrogen bomb test, which had an impactive force twelve hundred times as powerful as the bomb that was dropped on Hiroshima. For its remarkably abominable behavior toward the Bikini Atollers—who, beyond losing their home, suffered radiation poisoning—the American government eventually coughed up $150 million in reparations.

For a different trip across the Pacific, see *shanghai*.

bo·he·mi·an *n. One who lives an unproductive life justi-fied by art, or the idea of it.*

Appropriate to its meaning, the term *bohemian* entered English through the arts. It first appeared in Thackeray's *Vanity Fair*, but the subculture it described was most mem-orably portrayed in Puccini's *La Bohème*, which was ulti-mately based on a series of stories that were published in France beginning in 1845. *Scenes de la bohème* depicted life in the 1840s Latin Quarter and was written by Henry Murger, who, unlike the trust-fund poseurs inhabiting present-day bohemias from Williamsburg to Berlin, was an authenti-cally poor, deeply dedicated writer who died before the age of forty. Though the first to use it in print, Murger didn't coin the term *bohème*, which was Parisian slang at the time. *Bohèmien* had long been a synonym for "Gypsy" in French (as was *Bohemian* in English), stemming from a belief that they had either originated in or at least come through Bohemia, the Czech heartland of which Prague is the capi-tal. Murger and his fellow Latin Quarterites felt a special kinship with Gypsies, who lived a vagabond existence out-side of traditional society, despised by a bourgeoisie who saw their ways as a threat to their own and fancied them-selves to be the *bohèmiens* of Paris.

For more on mistaken beliefs of Gypsy origins, see *gyp*; for Bohemia, *dollar*.

breeze *n. A gentle wind.*

In an earlier time, when people paid more attention to the world around them, winds were an important topographical feature that created a sense of place. Old-world winds like the mistral and the sirocco still ring romantically in the ear. Zephyr, any gentle wind in English, was in Greece the light wind that came from the west. Trade winds were especially important; they were the fuel of preindustrial times, determining when and where travel was possible and dictating the seasons for war as well as for commerce. The Atlantic wind that blew out of the northeast and carried the Spaniards to the Caribbean, thereby making possible Columbus's discovery and the conquest that followed, was the Briza. Onshore, this same wind provided sweet relief from the tropical heat. "These hottest regions of the World," wrote Sir Walter Raleigh in 1614, were "refreshed with a daily Gale of Easternly Wind (which the Spaniards call the Brize)." Later English speakers applied the name of the trade wind to mean any cool wind off the sea in the tropics, and then any light refreshing wind whatsoever.

The sorts of storms that Europeans encountered in the new worlds they were exploring were as terrifying as they were unfamiliar. To describe the hundred-plus-mile-per-hour cyclones that regularly struck the West Indies, Europeans borrowed a Carib word, which English spelled variously as *foracan*, *urycan*, *haurachana*, *harrycain*, and *hurlicano*, among others, before eventually settling on *hurricane*. *Tornado*, while today mostly associated with Kansas, was originally a navigator's term used to describe the sudden tropical thunderstorms that popped up in the southern Atlantic. In the East, the monsoon was the prevailing wind that carried ships across the Arabian Sea from eastern Africa to India in summer and back the other way the rest of the year; it was the ceaseless and pounding precipitation that accompanied the monsoon in summer that gives us its sense of "a heavy rainstorm" today.

For what the Briza carried, see *cannibal*; the monsoon, *calico*.

bug·ger *n. A sodomite; in Brit. Eng., this can mean anyone.*
The scare that shook the Catholic Church to its foundations in the later Middle Ages came not from the forces of Allah being fought (and lost to) in the Crusades, but from a religious movement that sprouted up on the home front. Everywhere at once across Western Europe, heretics appeared; at first believed to be isolated cases, these men and women were in fact members of a network of fully formed underground churches. They were called *bulgarus*, the medieval Latin word for both "Bulgarian" and "heretic," an association owing to the Bogomil movement that had swept Bulgaria in the tenth century and that was undergoing a surprising revival. Although Christian, the Bogomil movement was cut from the same cloth as the dualistic

religions that had circulated through the East going back to Zoroastrianism. To boil the philosophy down: God was good and his realm was spiritual; Satan was bad and held dominion over all things worldly, including (and especially) the human body itself. What really put off the Catholic hierarchy was that the heretics placed their church on Satan's side of the ledger.

And not without reason. At the dawn of the thirteenth century, the Church of Rome was widely loathed for its corruption and avarice, while the Perfect—as the priests of the *bulgari* were known—preached purity, goodness, and asceticism and actually walked the talk, owning nothing more than the clothes on their back. They found a ready audience, especially in the South of France, where they were known as *bougres* (French for *bulgari*) or Albigensians, after the town of Albi, a hotbed of the heresy. The war that Rome waged against them was called the Albigensian Crusade, which by any standard marks a moral low point in Church history. In some cases, the populations of entire towns who harbored the *bougres* were exterminated; in more merciful episodes, only the Perfects were killed, being burned alive, dozens or more at a time. The Albigensians went back underground but were finally annihilated when the pope established the Inquisition, a move with centuries' worth of implications.

The French *bougre* entered English as "bugger," but how the term came to mean one who participates in anal sex is mysterious. It seems particularly odd considering that the Albigensians were ascetics, practicing veganism and not practicing sex, not only because it was considered carnal but because it led to procreation and the damning of other souls to the wretchedness of Satan's earthly realm. But many Catholics believed that Albigensians took part in the kind of sexual practices that don't result in offspring, which is maybe how *bugger* came to mean not only "heretic" but "sodomite." Or their enemies might just have been following that time-honored practice of bigots everywhere: When you want to discredit someone and don't have anything legitimate to say, just call them a homo.

bunk *n. Blarney, baloney, or any other euphemism you can come up with for bullshit.*
Life was not easy for a congressman in 1820 Washington City, not yet D.C. First there was the horror of the city itself, half built and located on a patch of malarial swampland that neither Maryland nor Virginia even wanted. Then there were the month-long statehood debates that finally ended with the Missouri Compromise. Pro-slavery, anti-slavery, everyone just wanted to get the hell out of the Capitol, and then, right as they were about to call for a vote, Felix "Old Oil Jug" Walker of Buncombe County,

North Carolina, got up to give one of his patented two-hour, go-nowhere, mean-nothing speeches after not having said a single thing on the subject when it mattered. Before Walker even started, all of Congress was hooting him down. Walker pleaded to be heard, saying, "I shall not be speaking to the House, but to Buncombe."

In that exact moment, a word was born. It was first used in congressional parlance: Whenever someone made a long, dull speech, he was talking to Buncombe. The spelling morphed into *Bunkum*, which by 1900 had been shorn to *bunk*, and in 1916 was immortalized in Henry Ford's quote, "History is bunk."* In the political realm, *bunk* was given competition by *baloney*, a favorite word of New York governor and presidential also-ran Alfred E. Smith, who is credited with popularizing the slang use of the word with sayings such as "No matter how thin you slice it, it's still baloney." As with *bunkum*, *baloney* is a phonetic spelling, in this case of Bologna, the gastronomic capital of Italy that must suffer the ignominy of having its name used to designate an American deli mystery meat that is something between Spam and an oversize hot dog, and such a travesty of *mortadella bologna* as to be slanderous.

Unlike with Buncombe, how bologna got to be associated with nonsense is a bit of a mystery, although it might have happened through the influence of a similar-sounding

---

* Which is not what Ford actually said, let alone meant, but no one much cares.

word that also came to the U.S. on the tongues of Catholic immigrants, *blarney*. Blarney is a village in County Cork in which there is a castle with a large block of bluestone that sits in a particularly hard-to-reach area atop the battlements. Anyone who manages to kiss the Blarney Stone is said to receive the gift of gab; because of this, *blarney* has come to mean smooth-talking flattery, or nonsense.

See *danish* for more on the confluence between politics and food.

cal·i·co *adj. A kind of cat, as in its coat.*

While Spain sought a route to India by going around the world, the Portuguese tried to get there by going around Africa. The circumnavigation of Africa was so daunting a task that it hadn't been seriously attempted in two thousand years (when the Phoenicians may or may not have accomplished it), but in 1488, Bartolomeu Dias reached what he dubbed the Cape of Storms (later renamed the Cape of Good Hope), and ten years after that, Vasco da Gama more or less finished the job, making it as far as Malindi on the coast of present-day Kenya. There da Gama learned he could ride the monsoon winds across the Indian Ocean; three weeks later he made India, reaching the city of Calicut in May of 1498.

The aim of the Portuguese had been to break the Venetian grip on the spice trade, and while Calicut was a major

Baghdad
Attabiy
PERSIA
ARABIA
Persian Gulf
RED SEA
Mecca
Mocha
Monsoon
ETHIOPIA
KAFFA
CASHMERE
HIMALAYAS
Shangri-La?
Jodhpur
Ganges R.
Taj Mahal
Bombay
Dungri
Madras
Calicut
SERENDIP
or CEYLON
or SRI LANKA
Arabian Sea
da Gama
to the INDIES-EAST
Malindi
Indian Ocean

Indian port for trade, its own native industry was cotton manufacture. Calicut cloth became the name for all manner of fabrics exported from the port, a term that evolved into *calico cloth*, and later just plain old *calico*, under which guise it became a generic name for cotton stuff exported from the East. In order to hide imperfections, the cheapest cloth was often dyed with bright colors and patterns, a look that the word *calico* became associated with in the U.S.—both as a kind of cloth with little flowers on it (particularly popular with pioneer women and quilters) and a cat with a lively patterned coat. In the UK, however, calico is unprinted cotton, what Americans call muslin, another generic name for the cloth of a city: this time Mosul. (Yes, *that* Mosul.) A couple hundred miles to the south of Mosul in Baghdad, the neighborhood of Attabiy produced cottons and silk called *attabiya* in Arabic, which gives us our English word *tabby*, originally used to describe striped silk taffetas and, later, striped cats.

(Another type of calico, dungaree, was made in the village of Dungri, now a part of Bombay. It was a coarse material, usually of a dull color, and often used for work pants and overalls, causing it to become a synonym for jeans.)

For more on jeans, see *jeans*; for Phoenicians sailing the African coast, *gorilla*; for the repercussions of da Gama's voyage, *mongoloid*.

ca·nary *n. A small yellow songbird; a prison snitch.*

Oddly enough, the most popular of avian pets owes its name to a couple of canines. Although visible from the African mainland, the Canary Islands were in only sporadic contact with the rest of the world. The Carthaginian king Hanno visited them on his great African voyage, a trip that was written about by the naturalist Juba II in the first century B.C. Juba is as colorful a character as ancient history has to offer, a Romanized Berber prince said to be descended from Hercules. Juba became a protégé of Augustus, who married him off to the daughter of Cleopatra and Marc Antony and set up the newlyweds as rulers of Mauretania, a Roman client state in the western part of North Africa. Sometime around 25 B.C., King Juba sponsored an expedition to find the Hesperides, home to the garden of the golden apples, a place guarded over by a gaggle of nymphs and their watchdog dragon. Juba's explorers sent him back a detailed account of the Canaries, which must have disappointed the king; it was mostly about lizards and a few ruined buildings. They did bring back to Juba a pair of large dogs, for which he supposedly named the main island *Canaria insula*, Isle of the Dogs, an appellation later applied to the entire chain.

The mystery of the Canary Islands lies in who lived there. Juba's report mentions buildings but no people; when European sailors began regularly visiting the archipelago in the 1300s, they found in residence a Stone Age people, later called the Guanches. If the Guanches had gotten to the islands by sailing, they had forgotten the skill, as each community lived in literal isolation. The Guanches, who succumbed in short order to European disease and enslavement, have been imagined to be everything from stranded Vikings to the last surviving community of Cro-Magnons, although DNA research now puts them as Berbers. The question of how the more famous indigenous inhabitants of the islands got there is less of a mystery. They flew.

For more on Hanno, see *gorilla*; for more on Juba's would-be ancestor and the Hesperides, see *Giants and Pygmies* (p. 64).

can·ni·bal *n. A homovore.*

The Canary Islands were the ideal point of departure for Christopher Columbus in his audacious attempt to reach the East by sailing west. Besides being the westernmost known land, the Canaries had, conveniently, just become Spanish possessions. Columbus's journey was daring because he was going against the accepted knowledge of the scholars of his age in the way he calculated the distance from the Canaries to Japan, which he placed at 2,400 nautical miles. The so-called learned men, who were using knowledge that dated back to Ptolemy, reckoned the world to be far larger. Columbus, as it turned out, was whoppingly wrong, and the so-called learned men were pretty much spot-on. (The actual distance is over four times what Columbus had calculated.)

The men in Columbus's ships, we have been told, were set to mutiny because they were afraid of falling off the face of the flat earth. The fact is, sailors knew better than anyone the world was round; by 1492, it had been common knowledge for hundreds of years. The flat-earth theory dates to 1828, the year Washington Irving's *The Life and Voyages of Christopher Columbus* was published. As he had shown previously, Irving did not mind bending the truth to sell a book, and he had no compunctions about spicing up a biography with some fictional scenes. That Columbus was a lonely and revolutionary voice in proclaiming the world to be round was utterly Irving's invention, and gave birth to one of the greatest historical misconceptions of all time. Far from worrying that Columbus would fall off the earth, his savvy crew more likely realized that India was just too damn far for them to make. Columbus's bacon got saved when he caught the luckiest break in history, running into one of the largest landmasses on the planet by sheer accident.

Columbus, of course, believed that he had found India, right where he thought it would be. Touring the islands he had run into, he began hearing of a local people called the Caniba. Upon hearing this name, Columbus believed they

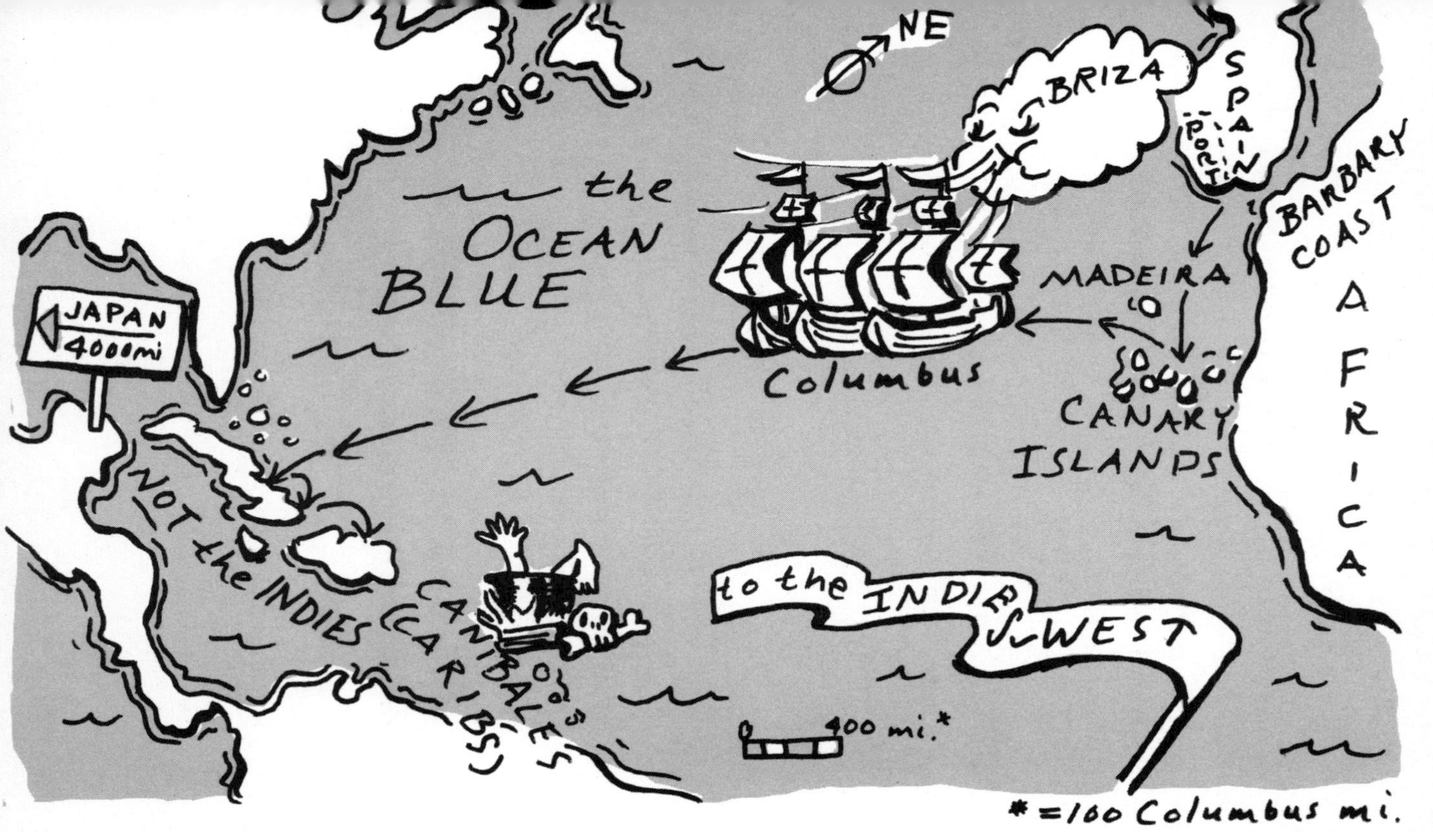
NE
BRIZA
SPAIN
PORT
BARBARY COAST
AFRICA
MADEIRA
CANARY ISLANDS
the OCEAN BLUE
Columbus
JAPAN 4000 mi
NOT the INDIES
CANIBALES (CARIBS)
to the INDIES WEST
0 400 mi.*
*=100 Columbus mi.

must have been connected to el Gran Can,* another indication he was in the correct spot. This tribe—whom the Spaniards called the Canibales—were also believed to be human-flesh-eating heathen savages, a convenient justification for enslaving them and stealing their land. (In Haiti, Columbus and his men heard a different version of the tribe's name, Carib, from which the sea and region takes its name.)

For more on Irving's fictions, see *knickers*; for more on Indies confusion, *turkey*.

UP AND DOWN THE RIVER

A couple of American expressions that seem to employ rivers metaphorically were originally meant to be literal. *To be sent up the river* means to go to jail; the river is the Hudson, and the prison is in the town of Ossining, from which comes the facility's famous nickname: Sing-Sing. A threat hanging over the heads of slaves in the upper South was *to be sold down the river*, meaning if they didn't act the way their masters wanted them to, they would be sent to the brutal cotton plantations that were located farther down the Mississippi River.

Another trip on a river no one wanted to make was

---

* Spanish for "the Great Khan," a wholly mythic figure; he was believed to be an all-powerful ruler and Christian, or at least curious.

across the Styx, the waterway that separated the worlds of the living and the dead; the ancients placed coins in the mouths of the deceased to pay the fare of Charon, the ferryman who carried souls from one shore to the other. The adjective *stygian* conveys the mood of the place: dark, gloomy, and hellish. A couple of other ancient waterways — these aboveground — have also become proverbial: one is the Rubicon, now an SUV, formerly a line not to cross that Julius Caesar crossed; and the Maeander, which was really, really winding. In crossing the Rubicon, Caesar was moving his troops from northern into central Italy, while the latter river wove through Asia Minor to its outlet in the Aegean.

Finally, there is the Rhine, to which we owe *rhinestones*. Originally, these were naturally occurring rock crystals collected from the Rhine riverbed, but they proved so popular that they were subsequently fabricated using glass with a metal backing. In the U.S., these imitation diamonds had their fashion heyday in the 1970s and '80s, with highlights including Glen Campbell's number-one hit of 1975, "Rhinestone Cowboy," and Michael Jackson's glove. The lowlight is surely *Rhinestone*, a movie that starred Sylvester Stallone and Dolly Parton and gives *Xanadu* a run for its money as the worst movie of all time, or at least the first half of the eighties.

THE CANTALUPOS OF ITALY

can·ta·loupe *n. A round melon of orange flesh.*

Here's the story: In the fifteenth century, seeds from a salmon-fleshed variety of melon were brought from Armenia to the summer papal estate at Cantalupo, near Rome, where the plants were tended to by monks. The fruit later migrated to the royal gardens of Charles VII of France, where it was called *cantaloup*, after the town of its provenance. This origin, or some form of it, has been repeated across dictionaries, encyclopedias, news articles, Web sites, and books, but it is problematic. To begin with, to which Cantalupo does the origin story refer? There are at least ten towns in Italy with the name Cantalupo, which means "wolf howl," or, more lyrically, "the song of the wolf." To us, the name sounds romantic; to the medieval burgher, it must have evoked the bleakest fringes of civilization. That said, the countryside makes a fine place for a papal estate, except that there seems never to have been a papal estate in any of the Cantalupos. What's more, what we call cantaloupe, the Italians generally just call *melone*, and not one of the many Cantalupos even tries to take credit for the fruit (nor do any of the many Cantaloups in France).

My guess is that whoever gave the melons to King Charles invented the whole cock-and-bull story just to make it seem like his gift was better than it was, the same as people have been doing before and since.

For another town that's hard to pin down, see *podunk*.

Cau·ca·sian *n. A white person.*

The Caucasus Mountains run from the Caspian Sea to the Black Sea along a ridge that represents the meeting of the tectonic plates of the Asian and European landmasses. Its most storied peaks are those of Mount Ararat, which loom large over the Armenian capital of Yerevan; it has long been believed that here is where Noah's Ark came to rest. If true, then all of mankind can trace its lineage back to this place. And since, of course, white Europeans are the uncorrupted race, they are the best representation of what the children of Noah — the original Caucasians — would have looked like.

This, at least, was the Enlightenment-mind-set thinking of Johann Friedrich Blumenbach, a German who divided mankind into five racial categories: Caucasian, Ethiopian, Mongoloid, Malay, and American, or white, black, yellow, brown, and red. He believed that the Ethiopians and Mongoloids — sub-Saharan Africans and Asians — had deviated furthest from the Caucasian model, with Malays (subcontinental Indians) and Americans (the other Indians) representing halfway degradations. Before you go thinking, *Here's another Nazi*, realize that Blumenbach's conclusions would've disappointed Hitler, as he argued vehemently against the inferiority of any race. He perceived racial differences to be pure aesthetics, variations brought on by different climates, which in a broad sense — very broad — jibes with what we know today regarding melanin, sweat glands, and so on. Blumenbach's main crime against reason was to set up Caucasian man as the basis from which all other races were corrupted. He did, however, believe that any of the other four races could revert to being Caucasian, if only they spent enough time in the superior climes of Europe. See *Neanderthal* for truly different varieties of humans.

chap·el *n. A place to get hitched.*
Martin was a Roman army brat. Born in present-day Hungary, he got stationed in Gaul when he himself joined the legions as a teenager. One wintry morning at the gates of Amiens, Martin came across a shivering, half-clothed beggar. Unsheathing his sword, the young soldier sliced his cloak in half and gave one part to the grateful stranger. Martin went on to have a saint-worthy career that covered most of the fifth century, achieving fame as both an exemplary hermit and a charismatic traveling preacher—a rare combination—and helping to convert the pagan Gaulish countryside before settling down to become the bishop of Tours. For all his accomplishments, it was the tale of the cloak that attached itself to Saint Martin as the symbol of his piety, and the garment's remnants became a sacred relic of the early Frankish kings, who took it with them on military campaigns and swore oaths upon it before battle; it was quite the good luck charm, as the Franks embarked on

a remarkable winning streak that culminated with Charlemagne's crowning as Holy Roman Emperor.

A traveling sanctuary held the *cappella*, as a cloak is called in Latin, and was attended by priest called the *cappellanus*. The fame of the *cappella* was such that it became synonymous with the term "sanctuary" in its sense of a place of worship outside of a proper church (or even within a church, in chapels located off the aisle). *Chapel* is the French descendant of Latin *cappella* (for the same reason a *chat* is a cat), while a *cappellanus* became a chaplain. English preserves the original Latin in the phrase *a cappella*, borrowed from the Italian *alla cappella*, meaning "in the manner of a chapel," as in to sing unaccompanied.

Cappella, incidentally, is derived from *cappa*, "a cape or hooded cloak." The Italians, connoisseurs of suffixes, add one to make it *cappuccio*, meaning hood, and a second for *Cappuccino*, which became the name of an order of monks who wore a distinctive sort of hood and who are better known in English as the Capuchins. It was another aspect of their robe—its color—that the mixture of espresso and frothed milk brought to mind, causing the name of Saint Francis's order to be lent to that best of all morning drinks, the cappuccino.

For more on the Franks, see *frank*.

coach *n. 1. In travel, a conveyance drawn by horses; a euphemism for a bus; the part of the airplane where you get to rub elbows and knees with your fellow passengers. 2. In sport, the guy in too-tight shorts and too-big sweatshirt.*

The horse-drawn carriage had a surprisingly short life span as a means of personal transportation, and even in its heyday was never widely used. From the dawn of man until about a hundred years ago, most people walked when they needed to get somewhere. Roads were awful; animal-drawn carts were for transporting goods, not people, while chariots were for war and sport, as was riding in the saddle. The wealthy, when circulating among the masses, had the option of riding in litters, or one-person sedans, which were used in England as recently as the nineteenth century.

During the Renaissance, however, carriages came into vogue among European royalty. Initially, these carriages were more grandly decorated than grand in terms of size or comfort, but the innovation of suspending the vehicle's body from its wheelbase led to a far smoother ride, as well as to the first cases of carsickness. One of the most glittering and worldly courts of the day was that of the Hungarian king Matthias Corvinus, and it was during his reign that Kocs, a village located a short drive west from the castle at Buda, began turning out the slickest wheels on the continent. Soon all the aristocracy of Europe wanted a "Kocs," which, despite how it looks, is pronounced *coach*.* Coaches represented an impossible luxury to average folk, and, ironically, it is this very status-symbol connotation that has pushed the term relentlessly down-market. It sounded so much better to call public transportation "coach"—it's what the queen rides in!—but somewhere between the stagecoach and coach-class air travel, the mystique wore off.

But how did it get to mean the guy in the hat with the clipboard? In 1830s Oxford slang, the tutor who carried you through your exams and delivered you to your destination (namely, graduation) was your coach.

For more university slang, see *philistine*; for horse-drawn vehicles, *stogie*.

co·logne *n. Male for perfume.*

> *I have discovered a scent that reminds me of a spring morning in Italy, of mountain narcissus, orange blossom just after the rain. It gives me great refreshment, strengthens my senses and imagination . . .*
>
> *—1708 letter from Giovanni Farina to his brother*

As the calendar turned 1700, Cologne was among the most cosmopolitan municipalities in Europe. The city on the Rhine was also a welcoming one, particularly for Giovanni

---

* The Hungarian *cs* is no more random a spelling than our own *ch*, as the sound emitted bears no similarity to the letters used; rather, it represents how *c* gets corrupted in certain situations, such as in *cappella* to *chapel*, as seen above.

DENMARK

POMERANIA

POLAND

•Hamburg

GERMANY

Neanderthal   •Joachimstal

•Cologne   BOHEMIA   SILESIA

Selters   CZECH REP.

•Frankfurt   •Pilsen

Baden Baden   •Budweis

•Rottweil   Wien•

AUSTRIA   KOCS•

SWITZ.   Lippizza   Buda

SLOVENIA   HUNGARY

CROATIA

RHINE

dancing horses

rhinestones

beer

Mitteleuropa

Caveman   spring water   toilet water

Farina, who had made his way there from the podunk Piedmont town of Val Vigezzo. Fleeing mountain poverty, Vigezzese immigrants typically plied the trade of *spazzacamino*, sweeping chimneys across Europe. Farina, however, had a different dream. Rather than clean their flues, he wanted to make Europeans smell better, a service they desperately needed.

Giovanni Farina first manufactured his scent in 1709, naming it after his adopted town and its place of manufacture. *Eau de Cologne* was different from every other perfume then sold, having a lighter fragrance. What was its secret? Bergamot. Bergamot is an odd little citrus fruit, kind of like a round lime but hard and fibrous and of questionable edibility. When you scratch the rind of one, however, you immediately smell perfume (or Earl Grey tea, which also contains it). Farina's product was an immense success and revolutionized the industry, literally changing the way people smelled; perfume today wouldn't smell like perfume without his process and secret ingredient. *Eau de Cologne* is still made in its namesake city by Giovanni Farina's descendants according to his closely guarded recipe and is a proprietary name. The general term *cologne*, however, is free to be used by anyone who wants to distinguish manly men from the users of perfume: The old term for scented spirits—*toilet water*—needed to be flushed.

For more on Europe climbing out of the Dark Ages of hygiene, see *seltzer* and *spa*.

cre·tin *n. An individual beneath you both in intelligence and social status; often, the opinion is reciprocal.*

Christians are cretins. Which is to say that our word, adopted from the French *crétin* after the Alpine dialect word *crestin,* comes ultimately from the Latin word *Christianus*. In vulgar Latin, *christianus* was a generic term for a human being, a meaning it retains in several Romance languages. It also meant something like "poor soul" and was a way of bestowing dignity (or pity) upon the less fortunate, which in the Alps meant people who suffered from an affliction that produced dwarfism, mental retardation, premature death, and (its most common symptom) thick, misshapen necks. Parts of the Alps came to be called the Goiter Belt, with generations of entire villages affected to the point where some believed the *cretins* to be a Pygmy-like race.

The problem was not genetic, it wound up, but dietary. People living in high elevations tend to consume little or no iodine, a deficiency that leads to hyperthyroidism. In 1801, this condition was given the medical name *cretinism*, which, like the similar term *mongoloid*, soon became a schoolyard taunt. But unlike *mongoloid*, *cretinism* has yet to be fully superseded by a more politically correct medical term, perhaps because the root cause was eliminated with such ease—by adding iodine to salt. So if you are a mountain-dwelling foodie who consumes only sea salt hand-harvested from the coasts of Normandy and you feel your collars getting a bit tight, better take a few shakes of the Morton's.

For more on little people, see *Giants and Pygmies* (p. 64) and *smurf*.

dai·qui·ri *n. The only cocktail that rhymes with* quackery *and* Thackeray.

Playa Daiquiri is the name of a beach in Cuba, which in one way or the other figures into the stories of the various people who claimed to have invented the drink named after it. But did the daiquiri really need inventing? It uses the ingredients most plentifully available in Cuba—rum, sugar, lime juice—and follows the same basic recipe as grog, which had been served in the British navy since the eighteenth century and was a popular drink across the Caribbean. The daiquiri is in the pantheon of classic cocktails, a favorite of both Hemingway and JFK, and in its proper form bears no resemblance to the spiked slushies churned out by frozen-daiquiri machines across the U.S. The first known appearance of the cocktail in print came, appropriately enough, in F. Scott Fitzgerald's 1921 debut novel, *This Side of Paradise*, which chronicled a group of hard-partying college students on the town in New York.

"Here's the old jitney waiter. If you ask me, I want a double Daiquiri."

"Make it four."

dan·ish *n. That thing that's been on the top of the deli coun-ter next to the black-and-white cookies for about a week.*

When Edith Galt met widower Woodrow Wilson, it didn't take long for romance to bloom. The couple met at the White House in March of 1915 and were married there before the end of the year, their march to the altar perhaps hastened by rumors that their relationship had already gone beyond what was proper. Washington wags said that Miss Galt was so surprised when President Wilson asked her to marry him that she fell out of bed.

The marriage of a sitting president was a sensational event; oddly, its most enduring legacy came from the cater-ing. Danish pastry chef L. C. Klitteng claimed to have used the nuptials to introduce his homeland's pastry to the American public. After the ensuing splash, he traveled the country proselytizing the joys and deliciousness of Danish pastry, teaching others how to make it and, if news clippings are to be believed, winning converts. Klitteng claimed to be a "patisserie savant" as well as the highest-paid baker in the world; whether he was a huckster or a patriotic Dane is hard to tell, but he ensured his beloved pastry's place in America when he convinced Manhattan restaurateur Her-man Gertner to start offering it at his establishments. The stuff was so wildly popular that Gertner got out of the restaurant business and started manufacturing danishes wholesale. (Which might answer the question many of us have asked: Are all danishes mass-produced at the same central location?)

The Danes, incidentally, call the pastry *wienerbrod*, Viennese bread, after the people who taught *them* how to make it.

dol·lar *n. Something that used to be worth more than it is.*
Currencies throughout history have been named after the places they serve, from the French franc to the florin of Florence. America, on the other hand, owes the name of its money to a town in the Czech Republic.

Prior to independence, the American colonies employed a farrago of currencies; far from exclusively using the coin of their British overlords or those minted by the colonies themselves, the global shipping trade brought in monies from around the world. Due to its control of the ex-Incan mines of South America, Spain largely controlled the market for silver, and its pieces of eight were an especially popular form of hard currency. (The term *two bits* refers to it still.) The silver Spanish coin was often called a *dollar*, a term that had become generic for silver coins of a certain value. The *daler* or *thaler* or *taler* was a popular name for currencies across northern Europe and represents a Germanic word meaning "valley," seen in the English expression *hill and dale*, as well as in place names such as Clydesdale and Airedale. But the "dale" of *dollar* represents the Bohemian river valley of Joachimstal, where the silver was mined for a currency first struck in 1519; the coin was nicknamed the Joachimstaler, and later just the taler. (Another coin named after the source of its raw material is that preferred currency of international villainry, the Krugerrand, whose gold came from the mines of the Rand in the Transvaal; Kruger was the name of the president whose mug graced the coin.)

"The almighty dollar," incidentally, is a phrase coined by Washington Irving, and attests not to the dollar's prowess, but its improper worship.

don·ny·brook *n. A rowdy, no-holds-barred brawl.*
Donnybrook, in County Dublin, Ireland, held a fair that famously degenerated into a series of drunken brawls on an annual basis. The madness finally ended in 1855.

fan·a·bla *interj. Stronger than* crap, *weaker than* fuck.
The urge to assimilate in immigrant families is usually strong, but it was essential in Italian and German communities during World War II, a time when the languages of both disappeared from the curricula of American high schools and their use was forbidden in households by parents for whom Italiano or Deutsch was the mother tongue. My father grew up in such a household, so what Italian he learned he picked up on the streets, making for a vocabulary heavy on the exclamations. Meals commence with

"Let's *mange!*" (from *mangiare*, to eat), sneezes are met by "*Salud!*" (which, like *gesundheit*, means "health"), and when no Anglo-Saxon word is strong enough, only a "*Fongul!*" or "*Fanabla!*" will do.

Fongul is a southern Italian corruption of the most popular and intense of Italian swear words, *vaffanculo*. Psychologists say that a person can only truly curse in their native language, as the section of the brain that stores taboo words stops absorbing at a young age. The most famous symptom of Tourette's syndrome is how it reverses this taboo filter and causes people to blurt out curses, one of the most popular of which among American sufferers is *fongul*. This either means that there are a lot of Italian Americans in this country or that we are particularly susceptible to Tourette's.

A milder curse than *fongul*, *fanabla* is short for *va fa Napoli*, which means "Go to Naples" (*vaffanculo* is a contraction of *va fa in culo*, which means to go someplace else entirely). It's a play on the nineteenth-century expression "See Naples and die," meaning that the magnificence of the city would kill you (an action more likely taken care of today by the Camorra). So *fanabla* means, essentially, Die! But what's it doing in a book about English? Well, the funny thing about *fanabla* is that it is purely an American expression. Italian American, that is.

For more Naples, see the desserts section of Appendix II.

fez *n. 1. A pillbox-like hat, but taller and tapering; often made of red felt, often with a tassel. 2. A late, lamented New York bar.*

The fez, though now purely quaint, has been a symbol of both modernism and backwardness. Although the shape of the hat is ancient, the fez proper dates to an 1826 law by Ottoman emperor Mahmud II that mandated its use among his male subjects. The emperor's hope was that the fez would supplant the turban, and was part of his efforts to modernize nearly every aspect of an empire that stretched from Asia to the Atlantic. One of its most westerly out-posts, the town of Fez, was a center of the hat's manufac-ture and seemingly the source of its name. In any event, Mahmud's law didn't help matters much, as the fez itself came to be a symbol of the exotic East. In this vein, it was adopted by Victorian Englishmen, who when at their lei-sure would don a fez, slip on a smoking jacket, and repair to their studies to read the latest Sherlock Holmes adventure.

Ninety-nine years after Mahmud II's law, one of the greatest reformers in history would resurrect the hat wars. Mustafa Kemal Ataturk had kept Turkey from complete dismemberment after its disastrous defeat in World War I. Like Mahmud II, Ataturk believed that one of the reasons for Turkey's weakness was its backwardness, and as presi-dent, he legislated revolutionary social changes, most sym-bolically the demand that Turks adopt Western-style dress and abandon the veil and turban. (Ataturk himself favored a Panama hat.) Lamentably, his list of prohibited fashions also included the fez, which had gone from being a hat of elegant simplicity to a sight gag in comic strips, thanks to those damn silly Englishmen.

For other things Turkish, see *turkey*.

frank *adj. Open and honest.*

A Germanic tribe that stepped into history around A.D. 50, the Franks would spend the rest of the first millennium conquering a good chunk of Rome's European holdings, and then some. At their height, the Franks held most of what today are Europe's French-, German-, and Dutch-speaking regions, and their influence reached further, as evidenced by Charlemagne forcing the pope to crown him Holy Roman Emperor in 800. Charlemagne and his knights were the heroes of the Middle Ages, and in their (idealized) tradition, their descendants launched the Crusades. The Muslims of the Levant, puzzled by these filthy barbarians attacking them, took to indiscriminately calling all Crusaders—and henceforth all Christians—Franks.

Among European tongues, words derived from Latin *Francus* were overwhelmingly positive. Historically, *frank* took on two senses. In the first, it denoted something of superior quality, a meaning seen in *frankincense*, the really *good* incense. In the second, it simply meant "free," as the

Franks were the only free people in their kingdom. Thus, *frank traffic* is free trade, and to be frank with someone was to speak freely and without worry of consequence, or giving a damn.

Whether the term *lingua franca* originally meant the language of the Franks or the language of free trade (or something else) is a matter open to debate. Though now deployed to mean any language used for common understanding (basically, English), the lingua franca was a pidgin used by Mediterranean sailors that was in essence an uninflected vulgar Latin (basically, Italian) with vocabulary borrowed from any language that touched the sea.

frieze *n. In arch., a decorative band, usu. sculpted.*
Rather than being an architectural border, a frieze was originally an embroidered one, in reference to an ancient specialty of the Phrygians. (The evolution of the word went something like *Phrygium>frigium>frisium>frise*, from Latin through to French.) The Phrygians were also known for their headwear. Looking like fashion for an elf (which in fact it was, for the Smurfs), the Phrygian cap was worn by freed slaves in ancient Rome, and for that reason was adopted as a symbol of liberty during the French Revolution.

Phrygia was the name of a land that through the centuries referred to varying chunks of Asia Minor, mostly in the interior. Its capital, Gordium, was named after Gordias, a guy who had the extreme good luck to bring an oxcart into town right after the chief oracle had prophesied that the next man to do so would be declared King of Phrygia. Later, Gordias's son Midas had the fateful cart tied up with an intricate knot in the palace, with the prophecy that whoever untied it would become master of Asia. (The Phrygians were big into prophecies.) This is King Midas of the golden touch and donkey ears, and the Gordian knot that Alexander the Great undid with one downward stroke of the sword, an action known as the Alexandrian solution. For elf fashion, see *smurf*; for another prophecy involving Alexander, *ammonia*.

go·ril·la *n. A large ape; in the eight-hundred-pound indoor variety, what no one wants to mention.*

The first great explorer known to history is Hanno, the King of Carthage who sailed down the western coast of Africa some time around 500 B.C. His journey is known from an account he left in his city's main temple. Carthaginians were Phoenicians, long the world's most intrepid seafarers; previous generations had already explored parts of the Atlantic, trading for tin in Britain and setting up a dye-manufacturing facility in Mogador, which sat on the coast of present-day Morocco. The reasons for Hanno's trip are obscure (his account was brief—it had to be chiseled), but the king had on his mind something more than a quest for knowledge, as he led a fleet of sixty ships carrying thirty thousand people.

Through the Pillars of Hercules the convoy sailed, passing the Atlas Mountains, to make its first major stop at Mogador to check on the colony. The cornerstone of Phoenician trade had long been Tyrian purple; the dye was extracted from sea snails, a task that was labor-intensive to the extreme but worth it for a commodity more precious than gold. In Mogador they had found a related species of mollusk, and Hanno likely was replenishing the colony, as well as establishing a new one farther south at Kerne. Kerne, which sat on the Tropic of Cancer, was considered the limit of the world; the waters beyond were thought not to be navigable. Most Greek and Roman observers thus considered the rest of Hanno's journey to be a tall tale. His account ends:

> There was an island . . . full of savage men. There were women, too, in even greater number. They had hairy bodies, and the interpreters called them Goril-lae. When we pursued them we were unable to take any of the men; for they had all escaped, by climb-ing the steep places and defending themselves with stones; but we took three of the women, who bit and scratched their leaders, and would not follow us. So

Pillars of Hercules

Mogador

CANARY ISLANDS

CARTHAGE

SARDINIA

Fez

ATLAS MOUNTAINS

Tropic of Cancer

Kerne

SAHARA

Taoudenni

Timbuktu

HANNO

Mt. Cameroon

Equator

WESTERN AFRICA

we killed them and flayed them, and brought their skins to Carthage. For we did not voyage further, provisions failing us.

Pliny reports that the skins were still in the temple of Baal, along with Hanno's account, when the Romans gave Carthage its brutally thorough sacking of 146 B.C. and extinguished the Phoenicians from history. The name *gorilla* was given to the largest species of ape by an American missionary in 1847, but as gorillas live well south of the tropic, it has long been assumed that there's no connection between Hanno's hairy savages and these primates. However, some historians now believe that Hanno unmistakably described the Gulf of Guinea and Mount Cameroon, which would mean he made it as far as the equator, a feat that wouldn't be matched for another two thousand years. It also means that his convoy did reach the natural habitat of the gorilla, and that the above account may be the first recorded human encounter with the animal. Not exactly an auspicious one.

For men following in Hanno's footsteps, see *calico* and *canary*; for Phoenician dye production, *indigo*.

GIANTS AND PYGMIES

Greek myth teems with fantastical races whose names have become proverbial, and nearly all of them, at one time or another, had to tangle with Hercules. The Pygmies, of course, were extraordinarily small, so much so that they were said to harvest their wheat with axes. Most famously, they waged an annual war with the cranes, who came to steal their grain. The Pygmies were long believed not to be mythological but actual; though they were often described as thumb-sized, the naturalist Pliny placed them at a more reasonable height of twenty-seven inches.* Their homeland was a persistent source of speculation, believed to be either beyond the Ganges or near the source of the Nile (according to Aristotle), which would place them in proximity to the African hunter-gatherer peoples also called Pygmies. These Pygmies, however, were given their name by Europeans who first encountered them in the nineteenth century.

A synonym for *pygmy* is *lilliputian*, which entered our language soon after the 1726 publication of *Gulliver's Travels* by Jonathan Swift. The book's most famous scene, in which the protagonist is tied down by the six-inch-tall denizens of Lilliput, was actually borrowed by Swift from the tale of Hercules and the Pygmies. Swift's book also was the source

---

* The name *Pygmy* comes from a Greek unit of measure, the length from elbow to knuckles. *Punch*, from the Latin *pugno* (fist), is a related word.

of the term *Brobdingnagian*, which has not endured, maybe because we have so many synonyms for *giant* already. The term *giant* itself comes from a mythological tribe of monsters, as does *titan*. The children of Gaia and Uranus, the Titans warred for supremacy with the Olympian gods, and lost. The Giants were a later generation called upon to avenge the defeat of their older brothers; they too lost, defeated with the help of Hercules, who in the course of his twelve labors would encounter the most famous Titan.

On his eleventh labor, Hercules was charged with retrieving golden apples from the Garden of the Hesperides. The Titan Atlas had his own labor, holding up the heavens, a task he performed in the mountains of northwestern Africa. Atlas also happened to be the father of the girls who looked after the golden apples, so Hercules journeyed to Atlas's post and held up the heavens while the Titan went and fetched him some fruit. The names of these two strongmen are writ all over the toponymy of this area, from the Atlas Mountains to the Pillars of Hercules to the Atlantic Ocean. An *atlas*, incidentally, gets its name because books of maps often had an image of Atlas for a frontispiece.

Labor number nine had Hercules journeying to the land of the Amazons to obtain the girdle of their queen. Again, the ancient Greeks believed the Amazons to be a real race; they were thought to have originated in Asia

Minor, where they founded various cities (including Ephesus) and fought alongside the Trojans against the Greeks. Supposedly, they either coupled with members of an all-male tribe in order to keep the race going or had male slaves that fathered their daughters; their sons they either exiled or put to death. Their fierceness in battle was legendary, which led to *amazon* meaning a woman of intimidating physical presence. The visit by Hercules ended badly, with the death of their queen, whom the Greek demigod believed had deceived him. Further proving to the Amazons that men were no damn good, they were next visited by the Athenian Theseus, who didn't settle just for the new queen's girdle, but kidnapped her entirely. The ladies, pissed off, invaded Athens but were defeated in the heart of the city by the very pig who had brought them there.

For more on Theseus and his abominable treatment of women, see *labyrinth*.

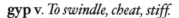

gyp v. *To swindle, cheat, stiff.*

To gyp someone is to treat them the way a Gypsy would, meaning to try to steal from them. This expression seems to have originated in America, which is odd, since it is one part of the West that has not at one time or the other felt plagued by Gypsies, their caravans never making it across the ocean in any great number. The term *Gypsy* is a corruption of *Egyptian*, the land of the Nile Delta having incorrectly been believed to be their homeland, a misconception dating to the time of Shakespeare. The people in question prefer the term *Roma* or *Romany*, which really confuses things, as they are actually ethnically Indian. Their language is descended from Sanskrit but owns a vocabulary largely picked up during the Roma's long, slow path of migration, which crossed through Persia, Armenia, the Byzantine Greek Empire, and the Balkans before moving into Western Europe in the fifteenth century. The big question is, why did they leave India in the first place? A highly speculative though romantic theory has it that the Roma were a warrior caste who in the 1100s met defeat in northern India at the hands of invading Muslims, who exiled them from the subcontinent and fated them to wander for eternity.

For another place the Gypsies were believed to have come from, see *bohemian*.

hack *n. One who writes quickly for money, often sequels.*
Hackney, once a rustic village on the outskirts of London, now a part of its inner city, was in the Middle Ages famous for horses. A hackney was a horse bred neither for work nor war nor even the hunt, but for the pure pleasure of riding. The hackney thus became a popular animal for hire,

so much so that the term grew synonymous with rented horses in general. As with so much else rented, the horses tended to be used up and bedraggled, and *hack*, in turn, came to signify woebegone nags, a term soon applied to other worn-out work-for-hire types, most especially writers and prostitutes. To writers, at least, the term has stuck.

Hack's earlier senses have not been entirely lost. The idea of horse rental was extended to carriages, especially taxis; in London they are still called hacks, while New York cabbies have a hack's license. In riding lingo, *to hack* means to exercise a horse. A good hack usually involves cantering, a word that, like *hack*, is shortened from a place name, in this case Canterbury, as in the *Tales*, and especially the pilgrimage. From Thomas à Becket's assassination in 1170, a trip to Canterbury Cathedral became a bucket-list item for good medieval Catholics everywhere. The usual route was the Pilgrim's Way, a path that cut across southern England and runs from Winchester east to Canterbury, a distance of 120 miles, though this was not the only road; Chaucer's gang left from a pub in London (or, rather, Southwark), on a route about half as long. However it was done, the pilgrimage—as attested to by Chaucer—was not a hurried endeavor, and the leisurely gait at which it was executed was called a Canterbury, or canter.

For London weekend ideas, see *Monumental* (p. 96).

BRITANNIA
dunce
cantering pilgrims
salt
'sport'
SCOTLAND
Argyle
Duns
Paisley
CLYDESDALE
R. Tweed
ENGLAND
AIREDALE
Isle of MAN
Derby
Rugby
Worstead
Worcestershire
Badminton House
Cardigan
London
Canterbury
Epsom
Sandwich
Cheddar
English Channel

in·di·go *n. A blackish-blue hue.*

Today our dyes, pigments, and inks are for the most part synthetic, but once upon a time they had to come from natural sources, be they animal, vegetable, or mineral. The original artist pigments were mineral, coming direct from the earth itself; the Paleolithic cave drawings of Lascaux, for instance, used ochres made from clay. Among the most popular artist colors are sienna and umber, named after the city of Siena and the province of Umbria. Ultramarine is another, made from ground lapis lazuli. *Ultramarine* means "beyond the sea," which is where lapis lazuli was imported from—specifically the Lazward mines of Badakhshan, a Silk Road region long dominated by Persia (and now dominated by Taliban). In Persian, *lazward* came to mean not only the rock mined there but the color blue itself; via Arabic, this toponym entered European languages numerous times, first in the Latin *lazuli* and later in the Romance languages, from which we get our word *azure*.

A prime example of an animal-based color product is sepia, which comes from the cuttlefish (Latin name *sepia*), a creature related to the similarly inky-sacked squid. Another kind of aquatic creature, a species of sea snail, yielded the fabled Tyrian purple. "The Tyrian hue," Pliny wrote, "is considered of the best quality when it has exactly the color of clotted blood, and is of a blackish hue to the sight, but of a shining appearance when held up to the light; hence it is that we find Homer speaking of 'purple blood.'" Tyre was the main trading port of the Phoenicians, who discovered how to process the mollusk, not a pretty job; it supposedly took as many as twelve thousand snails to make enough dye to stain the trim of a single garment, and the stench from the rotting sea creatures was so awful as to make the areas downwind of factories uninhabitable.

The most important dye after Tyrian purple comes from a vegetable, specifically a member of the pea family. Indigo was known from ancient times; it was originally called *anil* (or some variation thereof), and was so expensive that when Europeans wanted to turn something blue they used woad, an inferior local plant of the cabbage family. But the good stuff became plentiful and cheap once the Portuguese opened India to direct trade, and its common name became *indigo*, which derives from *indikon*, a Greek word meaning "of India." Most iconically, indigo is the blue in blue jeans, for which, see our next entry.

But if instead you are interested in dye-secreting sea mollusks, see *gorilla*; or, for indigo's role in artificial, aniline dyes, *magenta*.

jeans *n. America's pants.*
Fustian cloth was the first widely used cotton fabric in Europe, introduced by Muslims to the conquered territories of Spain and Sicily. Originally, fustian was not all cotton, linen being used on the warp (the base, as it were, that the cotton weft weaves in and out of). Its popularity was

largely due to cotton's softness and its readiness to accept dye. Because of its use in padding (for instance, to protect a knight from his armor), *fustian* came to mean superfluous, inflated language, a proverbial usage shared by *bombast*, another name for the cloth. Etymologically, the word is believed to derive from Fostat, a town just outside Cairo and an early place of manufacture. The fabric, however, was being woven in Italy as early as the 1100s in such places as Naples, where a kind of cotton velvet was produced that was called in English *fustian o' napes*, or *fustianapes*.

A cheaper, more industrial-grade fustian was made in Genoa; it has been conjectured—in all likelihood inaccurately—that it was used in the sails of Genoa's favorite son on his first trip to the New World. Although today best known as the home of Columbus, pesto, and a kind of salami, Genoa was one of the great maritime cities of the Middle Ages, on a par with Venice. Genoa is practically unique among major Italian cities in that our English name for it is not taken from French, as with *Naples* and *Venice*; however, this was formerly the case, when the city was called *Geane* or *Jeane*, and the fabric produced there *jean fustian*.

Jean fustian became popular in America, alongside the similarly sturdy denim, which was first manufactured in Nîmes, hence its original name, *serge de Nîmes*. Unlike jean, denim was colorful, and colorful in a particular way: While the weft was made of undyed cotton, the warp was stained with indigo. Because these rugged fabrics had similar uses, their names became confused, along with their qualities; this resulted in a cloth with the distinct weft-white, warp-blue face of denim, and the name of *jean*, which, when put together in a pair of pants fastened with copper rivets, became the all-time classic American fashion: blue jeans.

THE STUFF OF CLOTH

Much has been made of the cultural and symbolic importance of blue jeans, probably too much, but it would be hard to overestimate the importance of fabric to the history of world trade and economics. In the past, cloth was seen as better than money, an asset of intrinsic value like gold and silver. With the exception of spices, no product of the East was so coveted by the West, a fascination that began with the silk of China, for which the most illustrious trade routes in history sprang up.

Many fabrics are named after their place of origin, with more than one often sharing the same toponym; that, plus changing tastes and materials, can lead to much confusion. So although Marco Polo is the first European to attest to the stuff called *muslin* from Mosul, what he described was a rich cloth made of silk and gold that has nothing to do with what we call muslin today. Similarly, *damask*, which comes from an old English name for Damascus, has referred to a variety of fabrics associated with the Syrian capital, while the *madras* of Madras was used to mean everything from muslin to gingham to lace before becoming linked with brightly colored designs. Other names go so far back that we can only make educated guesses concerning their origins, such as *gauze* apparently coming from Gaza.

Less prone to change are the names of raw materials. Names of wools usually refer to a breed of animal, so we have *angora* and *cashmere*, goats from Turkish Ankara and Himalayan Kashmir, and *merino*, a kind of sheep bred by the Merini, a Berber people of Morocco. The trademark woolen cloth of Scotland is the *tartan*, a word with origins far away from the lochs and bogs; the term likely owes to the mingling of French *tartarin* and *tiretaine*, the former celebrating the Tartars, the latter Tyre. Tartan patterns distinguished Highland clans the way flags do countries. The distinct diamond pattern of the Argyll-based contingent of the Clan Campbell has long been adopted by preppies for their sock of choice, the *argyle*. *Paisley*, the name for that most psychedelic of patterns, also originates in Scotland, although the manufacturers of the town of Paisley were adapting an Indian pine-cone design they had seen on shawls imported from Kashmir. The word *tweed*, capturing the woolliest of fashions, results from a case of mistaken identity, as it seems a tailor mistook *tweel* (a Scottish alteration of *twill*) for Tweed, a river that for part of its run defines the border between Scotland and England. Worstead, a village in the northeast of England, gives us *worsted*, a more finely woven woolen cloth; a type of worsted made in Jersey, one of the two Channel Island bailiwicks, was a popular material in the making of a kind of exercise tunic, the forerunner of the sporting jersey.

On the continent, the Low Countries were famous for their looms; the town of Duffel produced a rough sort of eponymous woolen that, with a modified spelling, came to be applied to a type of canvas used in the U.S. to make duffle bags. Different spellings produced different fabrics—*cambric* and *chambray*—from the town presently called Cambrai, in French Flanders. Originally made from linen, a readily available fabric in those low-lying areas, cambric was later made of cotton and popularly used in handkerchiefs. South of Cambrai, almost to Paris, lies the town of Chantilly, famous for *Chantilly lace* (your pretty face), a staple of lingerie. Another kind of cotton or linen cloth was called *Silesia*, after the Prussian region of its manufacture. The cloth went by other names, including *Sleasie*, or *sleazy*.

For more on these topics, see *silk* and *calico*, as well as *beg* for some Low Country weavers.

knick·ers *n. British underpants.*

> DISTRESSING. Left his lodgings some time since, and has not since been heard of, a small elderly gentleman, dressed in an old black coat and cocked hat, by the name of Knickerbocker. As there are some reasons for believing he is not entirely in his right mind, and as great anxiety is entertained about him, any information concerning him, left either at the Columbian Hotel, Mulberry Street, or at the office of this paper, will be thankfully received.
>
> —Notice printed on October 26, 1809, in the New York *Evening Post*

The mystery of the missing Knickerbocker was a drama played out in the public notices of New York newspapers during the fall of 1809: "A traveler" spotted him in Albany heading north on November 6; ten days later, the hotelier of the original post writes of finding a manuscript that Mr. Knickerbocker left behind; at the end of the month came the announcement that *A History of New York* by Diedrich Knickerbocker was being published "in order to discharge certain debts he has left behind." The interest of the public piqued, *A History of New York* became a literary sensation and acquainted New Yorkers with a part of their history they had been but dimly aware of, the colony of New Amsterdam. New Yorkers began taking pride in their

Dutch heritage, and *Knickerbocker* started to pop up everywhere: as the name of bakeries, a hotel, ships, and even as what New Yorkers called themselves. What's remarkable about this phenomenon is that there had never been a Diedrich Knickerbocker, and *A History of New York* was largely made up—the man, the book, and the public notices had all sprung from the mind of Washington Irving.

Irving's guerrilla marketing campaign helped establish him as one of America's first literary giants, and also demonstrated why he would become one of its most problematic. His biography of Christopher Columbus was a huge bestseller, but readers again couldn't separate fact from Irving's fictions. In addition to giving New Yorkers a nickname, he gave one to the city itself: *Gotham*. Later, Irving would dust off old Diedrich Knickerbocker again, crediting him as the source behind "The Legend of Sleepy Hollow" and "Rip Van Winkle," the latter about a Catskills bumpkin who meets the ghosts of Henry Hudson's crew. These tales helped bring him fame in England, where a revised edition of *A History of New York* came out with illustrations by George Cruikshank, best known for his work with Dickens. The baggy knee breeches worn by Dutch burghers in Cruikshank's comic renderings reminded his British readership of women's underpants (such was the sorry state of nineteenth-century lingerie), so much so that underwear came jokingly to be referred to as *knickerbockers*, and, later, *knickers*. As a synonym for a New

Yorker, *Knickerbocker* has largely fallen into disuse, with one notable exception: its basketball team.

For more Irving, see *cannibal* and *dollar.*

lab·y·rinth *n. A maze that offers no way out.*

Once there was an island named Crete, whose King Minos asked Poseidon for his favor. The sea god gave Minos all he wanted, and sent the king a snow-white bull to sacrifice in his honor as a show of gratitude and faith, but the covetous Minos kept the bull instead. To anger the gods is never wise. Poseidon's divine vengeance became manifest in Minos's wife Pasiphae, who fell in love with the snow-white bull and birthed a creature that was part man, part bull: the Minotaur. To imprison this monster, Minos had a maze constructed that no one could exit. The great engineer Daedalus designed him passageways that zigged and zagged like the River Maeander and contained illusions to confound any man or beast. Such a good job did Daedalus do that he had trouble finding his own way out; his creation was called the Labyrinth.

Every nine years the Minotaur demanded to feast on human flesh, which the bull-cuckolded king fulfilled with human tribute from Athens, a vassal state of Crete. Two times Athens sent seven luckless boys and seven luckless girls to sate the Minotaur, but the third time, Theseus came among the fourteen. Ariadne, daughter of Minos, fell in love with the dashing young prince and gave him a ball of gold thread to unspool as he entered the Labyrinth. Theseus slew the Minotaur, followed the trail of thread back out, and—lousy lover—departed Crete, leaving Ariadne behind with her none-too-happy father.*

History has long been written by the winner, and all the more so in a fairy tale such as this. But there are historical origins to the myth, warped though they are by Athenian hatred of the Cretans and the human tribute they demanded. Minos gives his name to the Minoan civilization of Crete, a Bronze Age culture that was freakishly ahead of its time (they somehow had indoor plumbing). The palace at Knossos was a sprawling, multistoried complex with a mazelike and seemingly endless structure that may have given rise to the idea of the Labyrinth. Bulls were sacred in Crete, and earlier myths indicate that Minos *was* the Minotaur, the offspring of a queen and a god in animal form, a typical foundation myth in the Mediterranean. As for the end of Minoan civilization, it came not at the hands of Theseus, but likely on account of the cataclysmic eruption of the volcano at nearby Thera (modern Santorini) around 1600 B.C.

For more on Theseus, see *Giants and Pygmies* (p. 64).

---

* A ball of thread was formerly called a clew, also spelled *clue*; the clue in this case solved the mystery of the Labyrinth, and gave English an excellent word.

BLACK SEA
Byzantium
Gordium
Troy
PHRYGIA
LESBOS
Pergamon
AMAZONS
Ephesus
Maeander R.
MAGNESIA
PATMOS
Mausoleum
RHODES
the COLOSSUS
ASIA MINOR
MEDITERRANEAN SEA

la·con·ic *adj. Terse.*

Having conquered one Greek city-state after the other, Philip II of Macedonia sent a message to Sparta that went something like "If I bring my army into Laconia, I will destroy your farms, slay your people, and raze your city." To which his emissary brought back the Laconic reply:

"If."

Attic.

les·bi·an *n. A woman who loves women.*

The most feared Lesbian in history is Barbarossa, the pirate scourge of Christian Europe, but the inhabitant of Lesbos who turned the island into a byword for female gayness is the poet Sappho. Working in the early sixth century B.C., Sappho wrote lyrics in the most literal sense: Her words were composed to be accompanied by the lyre. On Lesbos, she kept about her a circle of females who have been imagined to be anything from a group of followers similar to Socrates' to a sort of Victorian finishing school with Sappho as headmistress to a cult dedicated to Aphrodite. Most of these scenarios are shaded with lusty overtones of girl-on-girl love, but it remains uncertain whether Sappho herself was a lowercase-*l* lesbian at all.

She appears to have had sex with a man at least once, as she had a daughter, and there was a tradition in classical times that she committed suicide after being left by her ferryman lover. This is generally considered a myth, albeit one believed by those who had far greater access to her works; we, sadly, have little more than scraps and fragments of her poems to go by, albeit enough to get a sense of Sappho as an artist. Girls and women are at the center of all her works. There is a bride who asks her virginity where she's going; her virginity replies, "I'm off to somewhere that I'm not ever coming back from." Sappho frequently addresses Aphrodite in her poems, as in the following:

> *Mother of beauty, mother of joy,*
> *Why hast thou given to men*
> *This thing called love, like the ache of a wound*
> *In beauty's side,*
> *To burn and throb and be quelled for an hour*
> *And never wholly depart?*

As for Lesbos today, it contains a petrified forest, one of the few in the world, and its economy is based mostly on olive oil and lesbian tourism.

For women who really didn't like men, see the Amazons section of *Giants and Pygmies* (p. 64).

lim·er·ick *n. A kind of poem, never serious, usu. obscene.*

If toponymity has a favored style of poetry, it is not the lyric but the limerick, which, beyond being named for a county in Ireland, usually has a toponym at the end of the first line to be rhymingly riffed off of. The master of the limerick form was Edward Lear, a superb zoological draftsman and ethereal painter of Eastern landscapes who is, ironically, best remembered for his verse and comic line drawings. First published in 1846, Lear's *Book of Nonsense* contains such gems as:

> *There was an Old Person of Rhodes,*
> *Who strongly objected to toads;*
> *He paid several cousins to catch them by dozens,*
> *That futile Old Person of Rhodes.*

Lear's poems are called limericks only retroactively, as the word doesn't show up in the language until 1896. (The name may have come from a poetry-reciting game in which every player had to end their poem with "Will you come up to Limerick?")

The most famous limerick, of course, is the one that begins, "There once was a man from Nantucket," which has become a punch line in and of itself, as the verse that follows is so outrageously vulgar. The original man-from-Nantucket limerick, however, was utterly clean. First published in the *Princeton Tiger* in 1902, it continued:

Who kept all his cash in a bucket
  But his daughter, named Nan,
  Ran away with a man
And as for the bucket, Nantucket.

Nan took it. Get it?

The filthy version, for those of prurient interests, can be found in the notes.

lum·ber *n. Wood, as in the construction material.*

The Lombards were the last of the Germanic tribes to ride herd over the Italian peninsula, a land they quite comfortably adapted to. That they are the source of the word *lumber* has nothing to do with the north of Italy being thick with forests, nor with a particularly prized "wood of Lombardy." Instead, it points to a profession that the Lombard people proved particularly skilled at.

Pawnshops have a long history. A way of mortgaging property on a small and seedy scale, houses of pawn were found in ancient China and across the classical world. Prohibitions against charging interest in the three great Abrahamic religious traditions curtailed the practice, although the interdict applied only to intra-faith lending—a Christian/Jew/Muslim could charge a heretic/goy/infidel all the interest he wanted. This led to the problematic notoriety of Jews as moneylenders in Christian lands; the more famous moneylenders, however, were long the Lombards, who devised a system of contracts with penalties and fees (similar to Islamic banking today) that skirted biblical intent. This led to the pejorative term *Lombard banking*, and from England to Russia a pawnshop was known as a lombard. The lombards would generally be restricted to a particular street (e.g., London's Lombard Street) and were identified by three gold balls, the flashing neon sign of the day.*

But how did *lumber* get to mean "wood"? Well, that's where it gets convoluted. The use of the word *lumber* as a building material dates to colonial New England and extended an earlier use of the word that made reference to useless junk, particularly old furniture—the sort of stuff you'd find sitting in pawn at a lumber.

mael·strom *n. A swirling kind of pandemonium.*

Today's preoccupation with nature is that man is destroying it; up until the twentieth century, the greater worry was of nature destroying man. Earthquakes, volcanoes, and tidal waves all fascinated in their horror, but for a sailor, the greatest, most unpredictable terror was the whirlpool. Whirlpools were the black holes of the day, but unlike those collapsed stars, abstract and impossibly distant, whirlpools were a present, earthly danger, sucking down boats, men, and even whales into the abyss. Charybdis—immortalized in Homer's *Odyssey* opposite Scylla—is the

---

*The capital of Lombardy, Milan, had a better reputation, and sellers of its expensive wares—especially hats—came to be known as milliners.

most famous whirlpool of all time, but whatever destructive force its swirling eddies once possessed were long ago sapped by earthquakes that reconfigured the shorelines of the Strait of Messina. The Norse had their own Charybdis, supposedly created by two slave girls spinning a magical underwater millstone, into the eye of which was sucked the greatest whirlpool of them all: the maelstrom.

The Norse name for this particular whirlpool, found off the coast of Norway, is *havsvelg*, which means "hole in the sea"; its more popular name was coined in 1490 by a Dutch cartographer combining *strom*, stream, with *maalen*, to mill or grind. The maelstrom gained fame as a popular location in nineteenth-century literature. Captain Ahab vowed in *Moby-Dick* to chase his nemesis "round the Norway Maelstrom," Poe visited it in his reportorial tall tale "Descent into the Maelstrom," and Jules Verne used it for the climactic scene of his 1869 classic, *20,000 Leagues Under the Sea,* in which a despondent Captain Nemo guides his immense submarine, the *Nautilus*, into the whirlpool's maw.

"'The maelstrom! the maelstrom!' Could a more dreadful word in a more dreadful situation have sounded in our ears!" Verne wrote. "From every point of the horizon enormous waves were meeting, forming a gulf justly called the 'Navel of the Ocean.'" The narrator of the tale made it out alive, but the *Nautilus* was never heard from again.

ma·gen·ta *n. Purple verging on pink.*

The Battle of Magenta was the decisive fight in the brief war that broke out in the spring of 1859 between France and Austria over the fate of Lombardy, a territory that the two had been trading back and forth since the French stripped the duchy of its independence in the waning years of the fifteenth century. This time, however, the French were fighting for the Italians, who bargained away Nice and the duchy of Savoy in exchange for French help in booting out the Austrians. The affair was as lopsided as it was short, the Hapsburg military being in even worse shape than Napoléon III's, and Metternich, the Austrian politician who had famously called Italy "merely a geographic expression," had to eat his words as the idea of an Italian state became a reality.

On another front, a chemist had learned that by distilling indigo with potash it became possible to create artificial dyes, which he called *aniline* in honor of indigo's old name, *anil*. Patented in 1856, mauve became the first aniline dye, followed quickly by fuschine. As news of the Battle of Magenta hit Europe, the name *fuschine* was quickly changed to *magenta* in order to make it seem like a more hip and of-the-moment color. (The original magenta, by the way, was decidedly more purple than today's version.) Magenta rose to the top of the color charts quickly, and in 1890 became one of the primary colors in the printing process

ITALY of THE NORTH

Val Vigezzo
PIEDMONT
LOMBARDY
Milan
Magenta
Gorgonzola Venice
Genoa
Parma
Bologna
Rubicon R.
TUSCANY
Pistoia
Florence
CHIANTI
UMBRIA
Siena
ADRIATIC SEA
TYRRHENIAN SEA
Rome

KEY
chimney sweeps
pawn brokers
pistol makers
Caesar
artist pigment

now known as CMYK: Besides M for magenta, K stands for key black, Y for yellow, and C for cyan, which is to say blue. Cyan was an even newer arrival to the language than magenta, coming from *kyanos*, a Greek word for deep blue or lapis lazuli; the same term is also the source of *cyanide*, a poison first obtained by heating Prussian-blue pigment.

For natural dyes, see *indigo*; for Lombardy, back up a couple entries.

mag·net *n. An object of attraction.*

The lodestone is literally the stone that leads; it freed mariners from the need to hug the coasts and opened the oceans to exploration. A lodestone is simply magnetite, a naturally occurring mineral; we just call it a magnet, a prosaic item in an age when you have them stuck all over your refrigerator, but imagine actually discovering the stuff.

It was the sixth-century B.C. philosopher Thales of Miletus who first noted the ability of the stone to attract iron, and that this property was transferable. Found in the vicinity of Magnesia, a city on the banks of the Maeander River, the ore was called by the Greeks *Magnes lithos*, "Magnesian stone." (Our word comes from its Latin adaption, *magnetum*.) The Greeks, as was their wont, merely pondered the mineral; it was the Chinese who first put it to use.

Records from the Han Dynasty (206 B.C. to A.D. 220) describe magnets as being employed by court magicians for the purposes of divination and feng shui. But by the fifth century, the Chinese had invented the wet compass. It is a neat trick: You take a magnet, rub it against one end of an iron needle, then set the needle inside the hollow of a blade of straw; placed in a bowl of water, the straw will line up along the north-south axis. With this innovation, magnets became lodestones. Of course, bowls of water in rough seas are not so good, a problem remedied by placing the needle on a pivot, the so-called dry compass. (The Chinese would often house the needle inside a carved turtle; for wet compasses, they used wooden fish.)

Whether Westerners separately developed the compass or got hold of it via Arab traders is unclear; who first used magnets to stick takeout menus to the side of the fridge is similarly lost in the sands of time.

For more on the Chinese, see *silk*; for more Maeander, *Up and Down the River* (p. 40).

mar·a·thon *n. An arduous and seemingly endless task.*
Professional long-distance-running messenger Pheidippides departed the town of Marathon to sprint twenty-two miles* to Athens to deliver word that the combined Greek forces had defeated the Persians. "We won!" he said, and promptly dropped dead. Judging from the annual turnout for the New York City Marathon, this hasn't turned out to be the cautionary tale one might have predicted.

---

* The distance of the modern marathon is relatively arbitrary; the length varied by Olympic venue until being set at 26 miles, 385 yards in 1921.

mo·gul *n. A magnate or tycoon, esp. of the media.*

Between the Portuguese landing of 1498 and the rise of British rule in the eighteenth century, the Indian sub-continent was dominated by a very different kind of foreign invader. While the Europeans pecked at the coasts, a devastating Turkic-speaking Muslim army devoured India from the north, a process begun by the first Great Moghul, Babar.* A descendant of Tamurlane and Genghis Khan, Babar considered himself a Mongol and aimed to establish an empire worthy of his forebears, although having grown up in Persianized Bukhara, his ways would have been foreign to his ancestors. (*Moghul* itself is Persian for "Mongol.") By 1600, most of the subcontinent was under the control of the Moghuls, who established an empire known for a wealth that was dizzying even by the standards of India, where the princely elite was expected to live in obscene luxury. Though in matters of religion they treaded lightly, the Persian and Islamic influence they brought to the arts can be seen in the Taj Mahal, the opulent mausoleum built by the Moghuls at the height of their rule.

Before acquiring its present use specific to titans of business, *mogul* was first employed metaphorically to mean a person of great power. A remarkable array of Indian titles have entered into English, as with *maharajah* for a person of showy wealth and *brahmin* for a member of Boston's

---

* His name would later be borrowed by a certain nattily dressed King of the Elephants.

aristocratic elite. *Nawab* was an Arabic term carried by the Moghuls into India, roughly meaning "governor"; in its corrupted English form *nabob*, it once enjoyed wide use to denote a person of moneyed extravagance, but is now mostly relegated to the more quoted than used phrase "nattering nabobs of negativism," William Safire's triumph of alliteration. The term *mandarin* originated in pre-Moghul India, where it meant a minister or adviser; it was carried to China by, of all people, the Portuguese.

mon·gol·oid *n. 1. A division of humanity ordered along racial lines, archaic. 2. A person with Down syndrome, archaic and offensive.*

The rise of the Mongolians owes to their mastery of the horse, the beast that allowed them to dominate their central Asian steppe homeland. Through these steppes ran the richest trade route in history, the Silk Road, which operated at its peak efficiency during the Pax Mongolica, an age when the Mongols controlled one of the most vast and well-organized empires in history. The Mongolians, sadly but understandably, were confounded by the sea, as witnessed by Kublai Khan's several disastrous invasions of Japan. The Age of Sail superseded any advantages the land-lubbing Mongols had, and (their Moghul cousins excepted) they retreated back into their steppes and faded into irrelevance. But their name lived on.

The identification of people as Mongoloids in a developmental sense was current in the scientific community until the 1960s, when the condition was renamed Down syndrome, which is ironic considering that Down was the guy responsible for coining *Mongoloidism* in the first place. *Observations on the Ethnic Classification of Idiots* was an 1866 paper in which John Langdon Down laid out his discovery that a certain kind of "idiot" or "imbecile" exhibited physical features that were identical to Mongolian ones. He called this a "degeneration" or "retrogression" from one race to another. What is most amazing of all is that Down was forward-thinking for his day, a proponent of the radical new theories of Darwin; Down didn't accept the division of humanity, and believed that if he could show that race was fluid—that a "disease" could cause a person to slip from one race to another—then he would prove the unity of the human species. Of course, using such superficial facial characteristics as eye folds to advance his theories shows that Down was a man of his times as well.

See *Caucasian* for another use of Mongolian, and *silk* for more road.

morgue *n. A detention room for the dead.*

In the first half of the nineteenth century, one of the most popular weekend destinations in Paris was the Morgue. Located not far from Notre Dame on the Île de la Cité, the building was styled like a Greek temple and allowed visitors the amusement of looking at dead vagrants under glass, naked save for some discreet genital covering. High windows provided optimal illumination, and the final clothing choices of the deceased were put on display for identification purposes, as the building's official mission was to recruit the public to help in identifying the anonymous corpses found lying in the streets or washed up on the banks of the Seine.

The original Morgue wasn't a faux temple but the dungeon of the Châtelet prison, a place called the *basse-gaeole*—basement jail—where Jean and Jeanne Does were temporarily heaped before being disposed of. Anyone who dared was free to wander among the scattered corpses with a lantern to look for lost loved ones in the fetid, dank cave. *Morguer*, an archaic French verb, meant "to stare at questioningly."

The term *morgue* replaced *dead house* in America; the Brits did and do prefer the term *mortuary*. The name, of course, was immortalized in one of the landmark tales of American literature, "The Murders in the Rue Morgue," in which Edgar Allan Poe concocted the genre of the detective story. (Rue Morgue, incidentally, is an entirely fictional street, but Poe knew how to trade on an eerily chilling name when he heard one.)

The names of several singularly striking monuments and buildings from around the world lurk within our language. One is London's Bedlam, the first insane asylum in England. Like Paris's morgue, Bedlam was considered a fine spot for whiling away a Sunday, when visitors could come poke sticks at the lunatics. *Bedlam* referred to the hospital of the priory of Saint Mary of Bethlehem, established in 1247; the name *Bedlam* was the colloquial rendering of Bethlehem, via the Middle English *Bethleem*. As a term, *bedlam* first referred to any lunatic asylum, and then to the sort of chaos associated with such places.

A more wholesome London outing could be enjoyed at the Mall. This Mall had nothing to do with enclosed shopping and chain stores, a post–World War II American repurposing of the term, but was a promenade through St. James Park popular with the seventeenth-century smart set, who used it to play the proto-croquet game known as pall-mall or, simply, mall.

One of the original Seven Wonders of the World was the Mausoleum of Halicarnassus. Who's buried in the Mausoleum? Why, Mausolos, of course. Mausolos was the ruler of Caria in Asia Minor, and in the fourth century B.C., he annexed the island of Rhodes, future site of another wonder. *Kolossos* in Greek referred to any giant statue, but *the* colossus was the Colossus of Rhodes, and the source of our word *colossal*. Built by the Rhodians in the image of their patron god Helios in the third century B.C., the hundred-plus-foot-high statue didn't make it to the second century B.C., breaking off at the knees during a massive earthquake. Even as a ruin, however, it inspired great awe, especially among early printmakers and writers looking for a ready metaphor. "He doth bestride the narrow world/ Like a Colossus," Shakespeare wrote in *Julius Caesar*, "and we petty men/Walk under his huge legs."*

Tall though the Colossus was, the awesomely narcissistic Roman emperor Nero had a statue of himself built that dwarfed it by some thirty feet. After his fall, Nero's monument was moved to the Flavian Amphitheater and its head remodeled into that of Helios, in honor of the Rhodes statue. The sight so impressed the bloodthirsty spectators filing through the entrance that they came to call the amphitheater the *Colosseum*, a nickname that stuck even after the statue was carted off for scrap in the Middle Ages. Nero's statue had originally adorned his palace; *palace* itself is a French corruption of *Palatium*, the Latin term for the Palatine hill, the site of Romulus's hut and thus the

---

*A third wonder was the Lighthouse of Alexandria. At between forty and forty-five stories, it was for over a thousand years the tallest building in the world until it too got done in by an earthquake. The island on which it stood, Pharos, became the term for lighthouse in Greek and Latin and remains so in French, whose word *phare* was adopted into English but has become so rare as to be extinct.

symbolic home of Rome's kings and emperors. As a name, *Palatium* came to be synonymous with the sprawling imperial complex Augustus built on top of the hill. Across the valley of the forum sat the steepest of Rome's seven hills, the *Capitolium*, later inspiration for another hill in Washington. At the summit of the Roman original was a temple, one part of which was devoted to Juno in her guise of Moneta, "the One Who Warns." It was here, somewhat curiously, that the Romans manufactured their coinage, and to which we owe such words as *monetary*, *money*, and *mint*.

One of the most impressive manufacturing complexes in history was Venice's Arsenale. Begun in the early 1100s, the Arsenale was the source of Venice's seafaring might, employing sixteen thousand workers, who churned out her massive galleys at the awesome rate of one every few hours. The name was a Venetian rendering of the Arabic *dar as-sina'ah*, meaning "workshop." The word *quarantine* also owes to the Venetians, from their policy of forcing ships arriving from plague-afflicted areas to wait at sea for a period of forty days, *quarantina giorni*. Venice practiced a permanent quarantine against its Jewish population, confining all Jews to a single area of the city called the Ghetto and restricting their movement outside of this zone. The rest of Italy soon followed with ghettos of their own.

Ne·an·der·thal *n. A person of boorish behavior and antediluvian demeanor; inevitably male.*

In Germany, close to the Dutch border, lies Neanderthal, the valley of Neander. "Neander" was the pen name of local seventeenth-century hymnist Joachim Neumann, as well as a literal translation of his surname, *neo ander* being Greek for "new man." It was a very old man, however, who made the place famous, or rather, his skeleton did. Found in a cave in 1856 by workers mining limestone, the skeleton was first thought to maybe have been a bear's; certainly it wasn't human. With *The Origin of Species* still in the early stages of being written, few people had any idea that human beings had ever been anything different from what they were presently. The first scientists to examine Neanderthal man believed him to belong to a diseased race — Cossacks, maybe. In a day when facial structure meant everything, the long-faced, heavy-browed Neanderthals were going to have a serious image problem. Especially once Cro-Magnon man showed up.

Twelve years after Neanderthal and again in a limestone cave, a group of five more archaic humans was discovered. Located near the village of Les Eyzies in south-central France, the cave was in the hill of Cro-Magnon. With skeletons that differed only in minor ways from a modern human's, Cro-Magnons were swiftly deemed superior to Neanderthals. They even had the caveman equivalent of the Sistine Chapel, the wall paintings at Lascaux. To the husky Neanderthals, these slender-boned giants with pinched faces who ran like jackrabbits must have represented the true first barbarian invasion of Europe.

The contact between *Homo neanderthalensis* and *Homo sapiens* has been the stuff of much fiction (especially by scientists). The Reagan years saw the development of the Neanderthal vs. Cro-Magnon genre picture, the first being *Quest for Fire* (which incongruously threw *Homo erectus* into the scrum) and the second the expensive flop *Clan of the Cave Bear* (which was largely an excuse to show Darryl Hannah in cavegirl outfits). But what really happened between these competing peoples? Why did the Neanderthals, after two hundred thousand years of species success, fade away? Theories abound. One is genocide, perpetrated by the Cro-Magnons; another is absorption through interbreeding. DNA research has just nixed this theory, however, while simultaneously confirming that Neanderthal–homo sapien hanky-panky did occur.

For explanation of *-thal*, see *dollar*; for cave-painting technique, *indigo*.

pan·de·mo·ni·um *n. Anarchy unleashed.*

Pandemonium makes its first appearance in the opening chapter of John Milton's 1667 opus *Paradise Lost*. Milton coined the term, which is a pastiche of ancient Greek and Latin: *Pan-demon-ium* is the all-demon abode, the unholy Stygian palace of Satan and his lackeys. *Paradise Lost* concerns the twinned tales of two falls: the first, of Satan and his fellow renegades' descent from Heaven to Hell; the second, of Adam and Eve's eviction from the Garden of Eden, as orchestrated by Satan. Although a godly Christian poem, Satan is by far Milton's most compelling, and most human, character. Upon his banishment from Heaven, you can fairly feel the wayward archangel's snarl:

> *Farewel happy Fields*
> *Where Joy for ever dwells: Hail horrours, hail*
> *Infernal world, and thou profoundest Hell*
> *Receive thy new Possessor: One who brings*
> *A mind not to be chang'd by Place or Time.*
> *The mind is its own place, and in it self*
> *Can make a Heav'n of Hell, a Hell of Heav'n.*

Having whipped his fellow fallen angels into a frenzy, Satan ends his speech with the greatest rock 'n' roll rallying cry of all time: *Better to reign in Hell, than serve in Heav'n.*

phi·lis·tine *n. A person wholly ignorant of the arts.*

It's a hard thing to be remembered only by what your score-keeping neighbors thought of you, especially when they wrote the best-selling book of all time. The only Philistine anyone remembers is Goliath, a giant who got done in by a pipsqueak with a slingshot.

Who were the Philistines? Their origins are mysterious, but they appear to have been one of the Sea Peoples who terrorized the Mediterranean world—most especially the pharaonic part—in the thirteenth and twelfth centuries B.C. Some of these Viking-like raiders eventually settled down in an area of the Levant that became known as Philistia, where they established a pentapolis. (Among their five cities were Ascalon, from which we get *scallion*, and Gaza, whence [probably] *gauze*.) Whoever they were, the Philistines assimilated into the people around them and faded away as a distinct nation by the fifth century B.C. Their name remained associated with the area, however, with the Romans calling their lower Levantine province Palestina, a designation revived in the 1920 Palestinian mandate.

As a derisive term, *Philistine* began life as seventeenth-century German university slang for *townie*, a meaning expanded to include anyone who lacked sophistication, especially in regards to the arts.

For other people of the Levant, see *bible* and *sodomy*.

po·dunk *adj. Of the hometowns of bumpkins and yokels, found from the boondocks to the sticks.*

Of all the one-horse towns that Americans have made fun of since the founding of the republic, Podunk is the only one to have been brought into the bosom of our language as an adjective—a podunk town. In 1846, Buffalo's *Daily National Pilot* printed a series of articles posed as "Letters from Podunk," a send-up of small-town life that exposed at length the importance of such provincial customs as the candy bee. (This is *bee* in the sense of a get-together to help someone, a metaphorical extension of apiary social networking that has passed out of use save for the spelling bee.) It is unclear if the author is referring to the Podunk in the Finger Lakes, a region near and dear to Buffalo, or had in his mind one of the various Podunks to be found across New England. There have been Podunks in Vermont, Massachusetts, and Connecticut, the last of which also had a tribe of Podunk Indians. The Podunks appear to have been named after the place where they lived, a boggy meadow; the term itself has been traced to mean "marshy place" in Algonquin.

Whatever its origin, "Letters from Podunk" was syndicated in papers across the country, and by the end of the century had become the quintessential town of the boondocks.*

---

* Boondocks comes from a Tagalog word meaning "mountain," picked up by U.S. military men serving in the Philippines.

NORTHEAST U.S. of A.

pol·ka *n. A kind of music, dance, and dot, all of question-able taste.*

Polka was *the* dance craze of the 1840s. A joyous sort of folk dance, it landed like an exploding cannonball onto the staid waltz scene. The polka was a little bit frenetic, a little bit sexy—you even got to put your arm around your partner's waist—and it captured a new age in which cities were exploding and revolution was in the air. It first infected Paris, where people packed houses for exhibitions of the dance, then struck England, and finally reached U.S. shores in 1844. Polkamania took the world by storm, with bars like the Polka Arms, a polka hairstyle, and even polka-dotted fabrics. Some thought the dance lewd and low-class, but it was quickly adopted by high society as well as the bourgeoisie.

Like all fads, the polka expired, except in the American Midwest, where large numbers of Polish immigrants identified with and took pride in the dance, the name of which, after all, means "Polish." The thing is, the dance has nothing to do with Poland; it was patterned on a Bohemian folk dance. There's nothing unusual in this: The Schottische, a copycat fad that followed the polka, had nothing to do with Scotland, nor was the Watusi, a 1960s surfer dance craze, related to the African tribe.

From a dance, the polka evolved into an American musical form, as practitioners began to combine faux

Bohemian folk ditties with authentically Polish folk music, as well as with jazz and other modern styles. It found a ready audience not only among Polish Americans and other immigrants from Eastern Europe, but with Native Americans. There is even a thriving Tex-Mex polka scene. Attempts to introduce American polka music into Poland, however, have thus far met with little success.

See *tarantula* for a very different sort of dance.

sar·don·ic *adj. Mocking underlined with scorn.*

If art has the riddle of Mona Lisa's smile, then literature has the puzzle of Odysseus's grin.

The scene is this: Odysseus has just come home to Ithaca from his twenty-year journey to find his palace packed with guys who have come to court his wife, Penelope, and generally loiter about. One of them, Ktessipos, hurls an ox hoof at the king's head. Showing Clint Eastwood cool and *Matrix*-like reflexes, Odysseus turns his head to the side and lets the meat hit the wall, flashing a smile the author calls *sardanias*. This adjective, first seen in Homer, has puzzled *Odyssey* scholars for thousands of years. The ancient Greeks connected it to the adjective *sardonios*, meaning "of Sardinia," and believed that the blind bard was referring to the grin that accompanied a particularly bizarre death ritual then practiced on that Mediterranean isle.

Although the idea that old Eskimos would float away on icebergs so as not to be a burden to their communities is a myth, under the Phoenicians old and infirm folks on Sardinia were done away with for that very reason, and not voluntarily either. Instead, they were fed an herb that perhaps seemed mercifully desensitizing, as it put its takers in a state similar to drunkenness and sent them into convulsions of apparent laughter. Thus intoxicated, the victims were dropped from a high rock or beaten to death. Seeing as the plant was highly poisonous, this seems a tad over the top, but as it was a method of dealing with criminals as well as senior citizens, maybe the violence was for punishment's sake.

Hemlock water dropwort is still a killer on Sardinia. About a decade ago, the dropwort-induced suicide of a shepherd who left a smiling corpse set off the research that identified this plant as the ancient herb in question. It grows only in Sardinia, and is a particular danger because it smells and tastes good, exceedingly rare characteristics in poisonous plants, which are all but exclusively bitter. Dropwort is also tantalizingly attractive when it flowers, looking like Queen Anne's lace or wild fennel, both of which it is related to. Our word *sardonic*, incidentally, comes via Latin, which also provides us with the medical term *Sardonius risus*, the locked-on smile that often accompanies tetanus.

selt·zer *n. Jewish for water.*

The bottled-water trade has a long history; up until the recent past, local water sources in even wealthy cities have often been putrid, and the only way to get potable water was to pay for it. One of the most successful purveyors of the trade was the German town of Selters, which had a local spring whose water bubbled effervescently. In the first half of the eighteenth century, the town fathers began exporting their naturally fizzy waters, and by 1845 they were selling two million "pitchers" across the globe, shipping it as far away as Batavia in Dutch Indonesia. One needn't get one's environmentalist hackles up, either; transported under wind power, this bottled-water trade left no carbon footprint (take that, Fiji), and instead of BPA-leaching plastic bottles, the stuff was shipped in tall, skinny ceramic jugs bearing the seal SELTERS. Early on, the second *-s* migrated from the end to the middle of the word,* and the water became known as seltzer.

Selters seltzer began getting serious competition in 1807 when a Yale chemistry professor started selling artificially carbonated water to the public. *Seltzer* competed with *soda* as the generic term for the new stuff, which, once flavored syrups began getting added into the mix, developed into one of the great crazes of the nineteenth century. To get in on the fad, department stores and apothecaries

---

* A process known as metathesis, the same reason why *ask* and *aks* have existed side by side at least since Chaucer.

installed soda fountains, which at one point outnumbered bars in New York City. Among the largest consumers of the beverage in its unflavored form were Jewish immigrants, who preferred the term *seltzer*, perhaps due to old-world nostalgia for German Selters *wasser.*

The original American bottled-water industry was dealt a body blow in the early 1900s when chlorine began getting added to tap water, thereby making it safe to imbibe. Although free public access to drinking water is one of the great successes of civilization, the world's thirst for bottled water has skyrocketed in recent decades. It began in the 1970s, partially due to the health craze—water full of chlorine and fluoride no longer seemed ideal—and partially due to a rage for fancy European mineral water, especially that bottled by Louis Perrier at his spa in the south of France.

For places where you bathe in as well as drink the water, see *spa*; for German water of a different kind, *cologne.*

ser·en·dip·i·ty *n. Happy good fortune, brought on fortuitously.*

In a letter dated January 28, 1754, Horace Walpole mentioned a discovery "of that kind which I call Serendipity," a word the author says he derived from "The Three Princes of Serendip," a fairy tale in which the title characters "were always making discoveries, by accidents and sagacity, of things which they were not in quest of." The story opens with the King of Serendip casting his three book-smart sons out of his island domain so that they may gain worldly experience. In their travels they come across a disturbed stretch of empty road littered with clues from which they deduce the following: A lame camel who is blind in one eye and missing a tooth passed by carrying a pregnant woman and saddle packs of honey and butter. The princes are later suspected of stealing the camel and taken to wise King Behramo, who asks them how they could know so much about a beast they claim never to have seen. The camel's lameness, they say, is evidenced by a dragged hoofprint; the one-eyedness, from grass having been eaten on but one side of the road; from gaps left in said grass, the missing tooth; the honey and butter from a trail of flies and ants; and the pregnant woman from a handprint (don't ask) and a good sniff of urine where she had relieved herself (really don't ask). Having obviously found some sharp (if weird) dudes, Behramo adds the princes to his court and they go on to have various amusing adventures.

The tale that Walpole read had been translated into English from the French rendering of a 1557 Venetian book, *Peregrinaggio di tre giovani figliuoli del re di Serendippo* by Christoforo Armeno, an Armenian who had adapted it from a circa-1300 Persian story. That tale, in turn, relates to an entire genre of Persian literature centered around Bahram V—King Berhamo—who ruled the Sassanid empire of Persia in the fifth century. Though not an especially distinguished king, Bahram was handsome and athletic and enjoyed the good fortune of reigning over a golden age. Persian poets spun tales of him for a thousand years, embellishing Bahram's meager accomplishments with old legends, including the one about the camel, which had been recounted in the Talmud (among other places) before Bahram V had even been born. The mellifluous *Serendip* was the ancient Persian name for Sri Lanka, a faraway and exotic isle.

Serendip was hugely important in the spice trade, being the land of cinnamon, formerly among the most precious of commodities. Serendip's location had long been hidden from Westerners, who took as fact another fairy tale, that of the Cinnamon bird, described by Herodotus as an enormous beast that collected cinnamon sticks from some undiscovered land in order to build its nests; the high cost of cinnamon owed to the difficulty in harvesting these nests. Eventually Serendip and its cinnamon passed into Portuguese, Dutch, and finally English hands, gaining another name, Ceylon, and being carved up into plantations for other tropical crops such as indigo, chocolate, rubber, and tea, as those who enjoy a cup of Ceylon may already know.

For another source of cinnamon, see *Heavens and Hells* (p. 141).

shang·hai *n. To abscond with someone unwilling and unwitting* .

Imagine you are one of the thousands of young men arriving in California in 1849, convinced you are going to stake the next million-dollar gold claim. If you are from the East Coast, you likely sailed, a trip around South America that took somewhere between six months and a year. Maybe you are by profession a sailor, or maybe you've never been on a boat before and were seasick the whole time. Whichever, your excitement is impossible to contain as you pass through the strait of Golden Gate into San Francisco Bay. In the harbor you see an odd sight: a forest of stilled ships, hundreds upon hundreds of them, all stuck here for lack of crews to man them. They say that every boat in America is going to wind up here, as even the most land-averse sailors have been jumping ship to head up into the Sierra Nevadas. No able-bodied man is willing to leave California, not even for the eye-popping wages you find yourself being offered as you wend your way through the docks. Just the idea of getting back on a ship sends a nasty shiver up your spine— you've been working all year to get here. Before you head to the mountains, though, you're going to treat yourself to some of San Francisco's legendary bars and bawdy houses. At some point in your drinking spree, things go hazy; you black out. When you wake up, it's on a ship. A ship!? You get an ache in the pit of your stomach worse than any you've ever had. You look back for California, but land is nowhere to be seen. You want to kill someone, but looking around at the rough characters on board, you realize the person most likely to die is you, with your body tossed overboard and no one back home ever to know what happened. You have to face it: You've been kidnapped to work the ship so that it can leave California. But where is it going? Shanghai.

Getting shanghaied was a very real phenomenon. It usually involved drugging, and the Mickey Finn of San Francisco was one Calico Joe, who was said to be so good at his criminal niche that he shanghaied cop after cop who had been sent to arrest him. After the 1842 Treaty of Nanking opened Shanghai to foreign trade, the city exploded in significance, becoming a key port at which to load up on tea and bales of raw silk. Shanghai was the most common destination for kidnapped forced labor because the ships going there continued on around the world; ports that were round-trip destinations had men willing to work its routes, figuring they could make a little extra seed money and quickly get back to California.

The age of the shanghai and enslaving sailors ended forever with the rise of steam-powered ships, which required far smaller crews.

For miners' fashions, see *jeans*; for nineteenth-century travel in America, *stogie*.

Vancouver
Seattle
San Francisco
SIERRA NEVADAS
XXX
Los Angeles

HAWAII

SOUTH PACIFIC

FIJI

←Shanghaied route   skid road   skid row

Si·a·mese twins *n. Siblings who are joined at the hip. Or chest, or head, or somewhere.*

It began as many great fairy tales do, with the king ordering the death of a newborn child. Or in this case, children. The poor peasant boys Chang and Eng were conjoined twins, and their birth was seen as a disastrous omen in early 1800s Siam. The order of King Rama II, fortunately, was never carried out, and his successor, Rama III, showed favor to the brothers, even taking them traveling with him.* These travels gave the boys a thirst for wanting to see more, and at the age of eighteen they left for a tour of America, thereby beginning a long and lucrative career as professional curiosities. In Siam, the boys had been known as the Chinese Brothers, after their ethnicity, but abroad they became famous as the Siamese Twins. (In early advertisements, they were also billed as the United Twins and the Siamese Double Boys; if only Doublemint gum had been around.)

Being joined at the chest did surprisingly little to slow Chang and Eng down. The brothers were remarkably coordinated, both in the athletic sense and in that they literally had to coordinate every step. They were also sharp businessmen who exploited themselves more than they let themselves be exploited by others, although P. T. Barnum certainly tried. As befits a fairy tale, the boys found their happily ever after, oddly enough in the American South,

---

* His own son, the future Rama IV, was seven years older than the twins, and would be played some 4,525 times on stage by Yul Brynner in *The King and I*.

where they adopted the surname Bunker, purchased a plantation in North Carolina, and married a couple of local girls who bore them a combined twenty-one children. Though themselves sisters, the wives didn't get along, so Chang and Eng kept separate households that they rotated between on a three-days-on, three-days-off basis. The Civil War brought financial hardship, as their Confederate currency became worthless and their thirty-three slaves went free, sending the brothers back out on the road. Returning from a tour in Europe, Chang, the harder-drinking and more garrulous of the two, suffered a partially paralyzing stroke and soon died. Believing a life alone was not worth living, Eng refused to be separated from his dead brother, and expired himself.

silk *n. A worm-woven thread of unsurpassed strength, smoothness, and sheen.*
Zhang Qian was an ambassador of the Chinese Han Dynasty who in 138 B.C. was sent on a mission beyond the Great Wall into the unfathomed deserts, China's version of Barbary. Zhang had an at-times harrowing journey, most especially a ten-year stint of enslavement, but the knowledge he brought back of rich cities, incredible foods, and divine horses spurred the emperor to open up trade relations to the West. What the emperor had that everyone else wanted was silk.

Silk was integral to Chinese civilization, its cultivation and production a closely guarded secret for thousands of years, with the export of silkworm eggs a capital offense. Within the empire, silk was at times even used as currency, and with the opening of trade to China's western neighbors, the fabric became a world commodity. The Silk Road opened at a very particular moment in history, when three great empires exercised control over great swaths of the Eurasian continent; in addition to the eastern Han, there was Rome rising to the west, and the Parthians of Persia between. To get some idea of how small the world became, consider that in 36 B.C., Roman legions tangled with Chinese soldiers at modern-day Bukhara in Central Asia. (The Chinese got the better of it.)

But how is *silk* a toponym? China was known as *Seres* to the Romans, and the people and goods who came from there were called in Latin *sericus*, from which we derive our English word *silk*.*

For more on China and the West, see *magnet*; for the end of the Silk Road, *calico*.

---

* To get from *sericus* to *silk*, drop the Latin *-us* ending and, ignoring the vowels, reduce the words to consonants only, à la Arabic. What remains — *s-r-c* and *s-l-k* — becomes identical when you consider that *r*'s and *l*'s change back and forth all the time (a phenomenon known as alveolar switching) and that *c* and *k* are the same sounds. Note how the Greek *aster* (as in "asterisk") and Latin *stella* ("constellation") are cognates with English *star*. *Serge* comes from *sericus*, too, but you'll have to take my word for it.

skid row *n. A street or neighborhood populated by the down and out; usu. in milieu of drugs, prostitutes, and pawnshops; often used figuratively.*

Although Skid Row is a neighborhood in downtown Los Angeles, other cities compete for the dubious distinction of being home to the original skid row. Almost certainly the term was born in the Pacific Northwest, where skid *roads* were common features of logging areas. Also known as *skidways* or just plain *skids*, these corduroy roads were made with logs skinned of bark and partially sunk into the ground over which other logs were dragged, or skidded. How exactly these roads came to be called *rows* and why the name got applied to seedy urban areas is open to debate. Some have offered that out-of-work loggers would hang around a city in such numbers that parts of town seemed like a skid road; others that the down-and-out would line the skid roads looking for a job. Seattle is often cited as the location of the original skid row in the urban sense, as is Vancouver, which had skid roads where skid rows appeared, including the notorious Downtown Eastside. Despite Vancouver's gleaming reputation as one of the world's most livable cities, the Downtown Eastside remains the site of a Dickensian squalor unmatched in Canada, with one of the highest rates of heroin and cocaine addiction on the planet.

slave *n. A person owned by another person.*

To give you some idea of how hard the Slavs had it in the early Middle Ages, consider that their very name became the word for "slave" in languages throughout the Mediterranean world. As pagans, Slavs had no rights in Christian lands, let alone Muslim ones, and so could be bought and sold like chattel, as they for centuries were in markets across Europe and North Africa, becoming the most popular breed of human for sale by 900. The supply was kept fresh and plentiful by wars and Swedish Vikings, whose constant raids into Eastern Europe were the scourge of Slavs. This sorry situation changed only when the Slavs converted to Christianity.

The Byzantine Greek word *sklabos*, meaning both "Slav" and "slave," was adopted into medieval Latin as *sclavus*. *Sclavus* replaced *servus*, the classical Latin word for "slave" and also a way of saying hi, an idiomatic use that came from the phrase *servus sum*, "I am your servant," an expression similar to the English "at your service." The custom survived in Venice in dialect form, *sciao*, and eventually enjoyed a revival as a fashionable greeting among Italians, who recast the word again as *ciao*.

See *Monumental* (p. 96) for more Venetian contributions to the English language.

smurf *n. A very small individual, sometimes blue.*

Remember the Smurfs? Those shirtless little blue creatures sporting oversize Phrygian caps who blazed to fleeting fame on Saturday-morning TV? Though a flash in the pan stateside, across Europe and especially in their creator Peyo's home country of Belgium, the Smurfs—or rather, *les Schtroumpfs*—are a comic-book institution. Beyond the fact that their name came to mean "little guy," what is linguistically remarkable about the Smurfs is their own use of their name to mean practically anything. Beyond toponyms— Smurf Village, Smurf River—the wee blue folk also used *smurf* as a substitution for virtually any word, from verb to adverb. (Their argot was severely circumscribed in the Hanna-Barbera cartoons, which stuck mostly to adjectives like *smurfy* and *smurftastic*.) So important was the word to their linguistic identity that a Smurf civil war broke out over its proper use.

The incident that unleashed the dogs of war in the 1973 tale "Schtroumpf vert et vert Schtroumpf?" was the borrowing of a corkscrew. When a resident of Smurf Village of the North asked a Southerner for a corksmurf, he was corrected and told that the proper name for the article was a smurfscrew. This sparked an angry debate across the village over the proper use of *smurf* in compounds and

the Low Countries

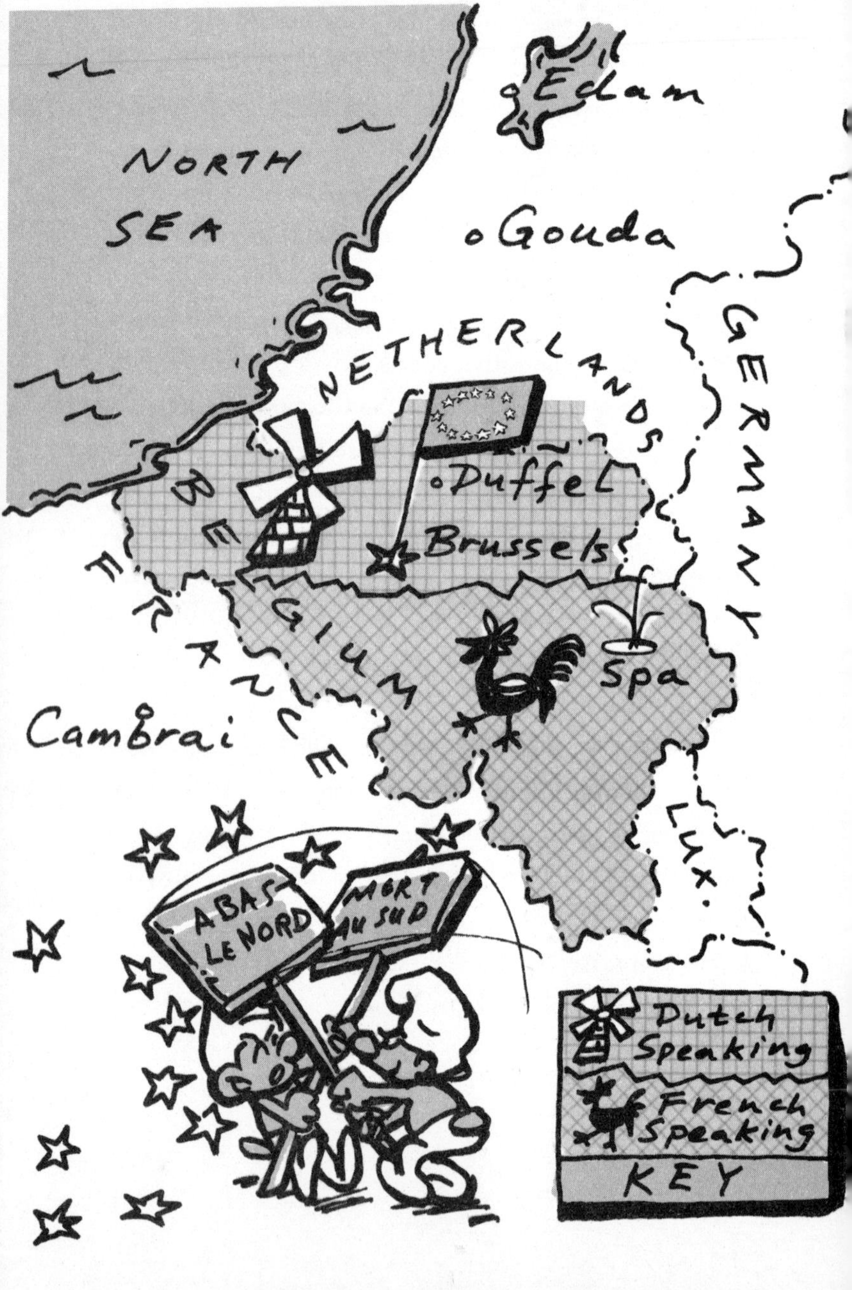

other constructions, with the Northern faction preferring back placement (a *mea smurfa*), and the Southern contingent insisting upon putting it in front (a *smurfa culpa*). As dissension escalated, a border was drawn down the middle of Smurf Village, dividing one Smurf's home such that the soft-boiled smurf he made in his kitchen became a smurfed egg when he served it at table. As ever, division sowed discord; Smurfs took to the streets with signs blaring DOWN WITH THE NORTH! and DEATH TO THE SOUTH! and began beating each other with clubs. The Smurfs united only in the face of an attack by their nemesis, Gargamel (whom they tied down with ropes, Lilliputian-style), but at the end of the tale it was clear that the language problem was not and never would be resolved.

Schtroumpf vert is a parody of the very real and scarcely less ridiculous language war that was then—and still is—splitting apart Belgium. Instead of embracing bilingualism, the Belgians have broken down their country into official areas where one language takes precedence over the other, an approach that has created a stark north-south division between the Flemish (Dutch) and Walloon (French) regions, a border that far-right supporters on both sides believe should be made international.

See *Giants and Pygmies* (p. 64) for smurfy inspiration.

sod·omy *n. (Chiefly legal) Any sexual act performed by a man that doesn't involve a vagina.*

If you haven't read the story of Sodom and Gomorrah since Sunday school—and then only in its genteel King James version—there might be some nuances you missed. To recap: God had been hearing a lot of bad stuff about the people down in the plains, and He decided that if He couldn't find ten decent men there, He was going to destroy their towns and kill them all. God sent down a couple of angels as his scouts, and they found Lot, an Israelite with a house at the gate of Sodom who had moved there only because the pasturage was good. The angels claimed to be out-of-towners, and Lot insisted on putting them up for the night and cooking them a nice meal. According to Genesis:

> *19:4 But before they went to sleep, all the men of Sodom, young and old, surrounded the house.*
>
> *19:5 And they called to Lot, "Where are those two guys you brought in tonight? We want some of that action!"*
>
> *19:6 And Lot went out the door to speak to them, and shut it behind him.*
>
> *19:7 And said, "Please, guys, that's not cool.*
>
> *19:8 "Look, I've got two daughters who are virgins; I'm begging you, let me bring them out here to you, and you can do whatever you want to them. Just leave these guys alone—they're my guests."*

19:9 And they said, "Get out of the way." And they said again, "You came here as a foreigner, and now you want to tell us what to do? We're gonna give it to you worse than those two others!"

At this point, the angels blinded the entire mob and said to Lot: "Look, we've heard all we need to hear—we're burning this frigging place to the ground. Take your wife and daughters and run for your lives. Go into the mountains. But don't stop, and don't look back." Lot's wife, unfortunately, couldn't bear not to sneak a peek and the Old Testament God, ever the stickler for His own rules, turned her into a pillar of salt. As for the two girls, they didn't remain virgins for long; with Mom crystallized and them alone with Dad in a cave, they decided to get the old man drunk and have sex with him. They each got pregnant and had sons. This, somehow, God was okay with.

so·le·cism *n. When you talk wrong.*
From Greek *soloikos*, "to speak incorrectly," after the people of Soli, who, although Athenian citizens, still managed to butcher the Attic tongue, mangling not just its grammar but doing so in a provincial accent particularly painful to Athenian ears. Soli was a city in the far-flung colony of Cilicia, located on the eastern shores of Asia Minor near Antioch, an area that was a backwater then, now, and in pretty much every era between.

spa *n. A place to get bodily services performed.*

The ancient Romans were mad about bathing, seeking out hot springs and establishing public bathing complexes called *thermae* across Europe; towns in this way founded include England's Bath, Germany's Baden (also meaning bath), and France's Aix (meaning water). After the fall of the empire, however, hygiene was more or less forgotten about in Western Europe until the town of Spa put bathing back on the map.

A Walloon town found in what is now Belgium, Spa became renowned in the thirteenth century for its hot springs. Its waters were not just for bathing but also for ingesting, as the minerals were believed to have great curative powers—no matter that the stuff stank of rotten eggs. Spa reached its height of chic in the eighteenth century, when going there became known as "taking the waters" or "taking the cure," and was seen as the best (or at least most enjoyable) way to get rid of gout or whatever else was nagging at the proto-Eurotrash that gathered there every summer. Competitors to Spa popped up, including Evian and the resurgent old Roman spring of Baden, now doubled to Baden Baden. Health was the last thing on the minds of many who flocked to these places; the social scene at Spa was such that it repulsed even dedicated party boy Casanova, while the roulette tables of Baden Baden put gambling addict Dostoyevsky into such debt he had to resort to hackwork to keep his creditors at bay.

England got into the act, too, with its first resort opening at a spring in Yorkshire, which came to be known as the English Spaw. Sadly, the spelling has changed, but the generic use remains.

For sparkling waters, see *seltzer*.

Span·ish fly *n. Classical Viagra.*

Beloved children's book author Roald Dahl also penned a novel for grown-ups. Instead of chocolate or a giant peach, *My Uncle Oswald* centers around a delight of a decidedly different sort: Spanish fly. Or rather, Sudanese fly, which the title character claims to be ten times more powerful than the Spanish variety and found only in a twenty-square-mile region north of Khartoum. Written with all the humor, verve, and maturity that marks Dahl's other classics, Oswald and his accomplice, the hypersexual Yasmin Howcomely, slip Sudanese fly to such great men as Sigmund Freud, Pablo Picasso, and Albert Einstein as part of an elaborate semen-stealing scheme.

While Sudanese fly is Dahl's creation, Spanish fly is quite real, although the insect that is dried and ground up into a powder is not a fly but a rather handsome beetle of iridescent emerald hue. Knowledge of the properties of the cantharis or blister beetle, as the bug has also been known, dates at least as far back as the fifth century B.C. and the Greek physician Hippocrates, and as a pharmaceutical it was used to remove warts and in getting stallions to mate. Whether or not cantharis should properly be termed an aphrodisiac depends on what turns you on. In its pharmaceutical form, Spanish fly is a stimulant that brings on priapism, a prolonged swelling of the genitals, and is so powerful that the line between dose and overdose is dangerously tricky to navigate, as it can bring on permanent kidney damage and other ill effects. The most famous case of Spanish-fly poisoning involves the Marquis de Sade, who was sentenced to death in Marseille for slipping it in pastille form to a pair of prostitutes. Sadly, the demented de Sade escaped to perpetrate further crimes, most egregiously against literature.

sto·gie *n. A cigar.*

Conestoga wagons plied the roads of America from its colonial days, handling most of the cargo trade along the Eastern Seaboard until the canal-building frenzy of the early nineteenth century. They were shaped like boats, with their bottoms curved and sides pitched so as to keep the cargo from spilling out. At over twenty feet in length and stacked as high as eleven feet, these wagons could haul as much as eight tons and took a team of a half-dozen draft horses to pull them. Their early manufacture and use is connected to Conestoga, a tiny community in Lancaster County in the heart of the German-speaking Pennsylvania Dutch region. A family of German blacksmiths, the Studebakers, became a top maker of Conestogas, and would be the only wagon manufacturer to successfully navigate the transition to horseless carriages.

The Stogas, as the wagons were nicknamed, were not themselves for passengers; people of means would take the stagecoach, while the rest of us just walked. The only men who rode these wagons were the hard-bitten teamsters driving them. They were iconic figures who favored foot-long cigars made of cheap tobacco that came to be called Stogy cigars, and, later, just plain ol' stogies.

sto·ic *n. One who suffers pain (and not fools) gladly.*

If you dream of becoming a movie star, you go to L.A.; if you dream of becoming a philosopher, you go to Athens. Or at least that's what you did in the early fourth century B.C., when a young Phoenician named Zeno left his island homeland of Cyprus to come to the big city. But what sort of philosopher to become? Athens offered a plethora of choices, among them the Academic, Peripatetic, and Skeptic schools. The Eclectic school, which would've allowed Zeno to pick and choose his favorite bits from the various philosophies, didn't exist yet, nor did Epicureanism, which would come to Athens in a few years. But Epicurus wouldn't have appealed to Zeno anyway; he was a serious and not overly fun guy who decided to join the ascetic Cynics before striking out on his own.

Zeno believed that happiness—such as it could be—was achieved through reason and virtue. He preached his philosophy in the agora, the central square of Athens where the main business of city life—from the public assembly to the marketplace—was carried out. (*Agoraphobia* is fear of such a place.) His main haunt there was the Stoa Poikile, also known as the Painted Porch. Calling a *stoa* a porch is a bit of a misnomer; it was a kind of grand colonnaded hall, with the Stoa Poikile being the most important one in Athens. Its "Painted" appellation comes from its murals, which depicted the defeat of the Amazons at Athens, the taking of Troy, the Battle of Marathon, and the first Athenian victory over Sparta. It was from teaching at this *stoa* that Zeno's rigid philosophy got the name *Stoicism*, which would later become of particular appeal to old-school Romans and, much later, stiff-upper-lip Englishmen.

For the stories behind the murals, see *Giants and Pygmies* (p. 64), *trojan*, *marathon*, and *attic*.

syb·a·rite *n. One deemed having too good of a time by those not having much of any.*

Magna Graecia was the New World of Ancient Greece. The original Hellenistic city-states began establishing outposts on the coasts of Italy in the eighth century B.C., colonies that almost immediately began to outstrip their homelands in wealth and power. Foremost among these burgeoning powers was Sybaris.

Sybaris was the Sodom of the classical world in its reputation for god(s)less decadence. Of the two damned and doomed cities, the title of more distinguished proverbial accomplishment must go to Sybaris: It wasn't all that hard to become the byword for luxury and excess by the standards of the dour Israelites and the Old Testament god they prayed to; to party too hard in the eyes of the Dionysus-worshipping Greeks took some serious doing. Rather than having sumptuary laws against extravagant displays of wealth, in Sybaris they awarded prizes for it; one Sybarite was said to be so rich, he owned a thousand slaves. The citizens of the town were derided by rivals for their general lack of manliness and love of little yapping Maltese dogs in particular. Sybarites hated athletics and wouldn't go to the Olympic games, a sin in Greek eyes. Instead, they trained horses to dance to flute music.

The opposite of Sybaris was Croton, its nearest neighbor and poorer rival. Croton was legendary for its athletes; its favorite son, Milo, was considered the greatest Olympian in history, having won the wrestling title at five consecutive Olympiads and being seen as a latter-day Hercules. They also had Pythagoras. Although best known for a theorem mistakenly attributed to him, Pythagoras was a New Agey cult leader, preaching vegetarianism and the healing power of music as well as claiming to know the secrets of reincarnation. He and his followers (of which Milo was one) took power in Croton and destabilized politics across Magna Graecia. After a coup in Sybaris, many of its leading citizens fled to Croton; Croton's (and Pythagoras's) refusal to return the refugees led to war. How the heavily outnumbered men of Croton defeated their nemesis is the source of many stories. One is that Milo, dressed as Hercules, single-handedly won the day. Another is that the Crotonese put flute players on the front lines, and when the cavalry charged, they started playing a tune, which caused the Sybarite steeds to stop and dance, throwing the attack into turmoil. However it happened, the Crotonese put the Sybarites to the sword and diverted the River Crathis so that it flowed into Sybaris and destroyed the city forever.

See Appendix I for more dancing horses.

ta·ran·tu·la *n. A spider that bites.*

Just up the coast from Sybaris, where the heel of Italy meets the instep of the boot, is another Magna Graecia city, Taranto. Taranto was for so long infested with a particular variety of spider that the eight-legged creature came to be known as the tarantula. This is not the big hairy spider you are likely thinking of—those carnivorous arachnids of the American tropics borrowed the name—but a rather punier and less hirsute cousin also known as the Mediterranean wolf spider. Although its bite is no more dangerous or painful than that of a bee, it was long believed to bring on

ADRIATIC SEA

Rome

Avernus

Naples

Brindisi

Taranto

Otranto

Sybaris

TYRRHENIAN SEA

CRATHIS

Croton

STRAIT OF MESSINA

Scylla

IONIAN SEA

Charybdis

Marsala

SICILY

ITALY OF THE SOUTH

◎ whirlpool

🕷 tarantulas

🔥 entrance to Hell

a severe psychotic disorder called tarantism that in southern Italy became an epidemic. The only cure for tarantism, which bedeviled females almost exclusively, was an ecstatic form of dancing called the tarantella, in which the afflicted vigorously tried to shake out the venom. Tarantism could be a chronic disease, with annual relapses stretching across decades. Although the tarantella is today seen as a kind of Italian polka, it appears to have been somehow connected to the dance manias of Europe that began around the time of the Black Death in Germany and would continue to erupt across the continent for centuries. Essentially, a group of people, again female, would go into a trance and dance until they either passed out exhausted, or died. The church considered the dancers to be possessed by the devil.

There are many theories about tarantism, and most conclude that the spider bite was a cover story for an ecstatic cult ritual. Most intriguing is the theory that the tarantella has its roots in the Greek Bacchanalia, implausible as it may seem. However, pagan rituals have persisted across southern Italy, sometimes merging with church rites (several towns have springtime festivals that preserve aspects of the Persephone cult), while the Lombard duchy of Benevento has long been famous for its witches, who are Roman goddesses in thin disguise.

See *turkey* for another old-world breed applied to a new-world cousin, and *beg* for women performing non-church-sanctioned activities.

Tim·buk·tu *n. The farthest possible place away.*

Though idiomatically the end of the Earth, Timbuktu once sat at the crossroads of one of the world's great trading networks. Located in the heart of western Africa, Timbuktu was a market hub for so-called yellow, black, and white gold, i.e., the gold and slaves of Guinea and the salt of the Taoudenni mines. In an age when Europe was just emerging from the Middle Ages, sub-Saharan Timbuktu was one of the world's great cities. Its initial fame came as a faraway land of unimaginable wealth, an idea with origins in the 1326 pilgrimage of King Mansa Musa to Mecca; reports place his retinue at sixty thousand people, with an additional five hundred slaves said to be carrying hundreds or even thousands of pounds of gold. Myths grew that the king was so free with his wealth that he depressed the currency of any country in which he sojourned, and that the streets of Timbuktu were paved with gold and even its roofs made of the stuff. (The roads, in fact, were dirt, and the most popular building material was mud; the gold, presumably, was kept under lock and key.) However, the true wealth of Timbuktu—at least to those who lived there—lay in its books.

When Mansa Musa established Timbuktu as the capital of his kingdom, he also established the great madrassa of Sankore. By the end of the king's reign, it had developed into one of the largest universities in the world, with twenty-five thousand students and a library containing approximately seven hundred thousand manuscripts. The manuscript-copying industry thrived in Timbuktu like nowhere else, in part because books became a status symbol like fine houses or clothing in other places. The opening of sea routes by the Portuguese doomed the importance of the Saharan trade nexus, but the manuscripts remained treasures to be handed down through the generations. There still exist about seventy private libraries and one hundred thousand manuscripts in the town, many reaching back to Musa's time, and it is hoped that this intellectual gold can rescue the once-great city from oblivion. Sadly, at present most tourists come to get their passports stamped, and leave.

tro·jan *n. A condom.*

It is the most famous episode of the Trojan war, and yet it does not appear in the *Iliad*. Instead, the standard account of the wily Odysseus's wooden-horse trick is found in Virgil's *Aeneid*, which includes the famous unheeded advice: *Beware Greeks bearing gifts.** As an expression, a *Trojan horse* has become proverbial for a nasty surprise that's hidden inside; as the name of a condom, Trojan stands unrivaled as a stroke of branding genius.

See *frieze* for the kind of cap Trojans themselves wore.

---

*The actual line, said by Laocoön, was *"Timeo Danaos et dona ferentes,"* which is closer to "I fear the Greeks, even when bringing gifts."

tur·key *n. A Thanksgiving martyr.*

For about 2,600 years after Odysseus's successful subterfuge, the Greeks remained firmly entrenched in the former land of Troy, until the arrival of the Ottoman Turks. Bad news for Greeks, good news for the English language, as the Turks have yielded us a bounty of toponymous terms. Many of these date to the century leading up to the Ottoman Empire's Great War demise, when so-called exotic Oriental customs became faddish and Turkish baths, coffee, delights, and cigarettes grew popular, as well as that kind of furniture known as an ottoman and the ridiculous habit of Victorian gentlemen wearing a fez while in repose.

The oddest application of *Turkey* is surely to the fowl served at Thanksgiving, a bird so American that Ben Franklin favored it over the bald eagle as the national symbol. The English had a meat bird called the *turkey cock* or *turkey hen*, an African species that possibly got its name from Turkish merchants who exported the creature into central Europe. When the Portuguese began bringing the same bird into Europe from the Guinea coast, it attained a second name, *Guinea fowl*. Meanwhile, in the 1520s the Spaniards began importing into Europe a related bird that had been domesticated by the Aztecs; Englishmen confused this new-world arrival with the turkey cock, and presumably the Guinea fowl as well. However, early-sixteenth-century geographical knowledge being what it was, people still believed that the Spaniards were bringing all this stuff back from India, which—if you're living in the English country-side—seems like pretty much the same place as Turkey. For more on silly Englishmen wearing fezzes, see *fez*.

tux·e·do *n. The only piece of rented clothing most men will ever have to wear.*

Considering that it is synonymous with formal wear today, it's hard to believe that the tuxedo began life as a casual alternative, but such was the nineteenth century, the era of uncomfortable fashion. While much is made of the way women had to truss themselves up, men didn't have it easy either. They wore shirts with detachable collars, both items starched to the consistency of concrete; over their shirts were strapped snug waistcoats and on top of that, black tailcoats that hung awkwardly long in back. This was evening wear, meant for every evening, even when you were just having dinner at home with the wife in the middle of summer.

Queen Victoria's eldest son, Edward, wasn't the formal type, and he designed for himself a more sporty sort of coat that he wore at his country estate at Cowes. In the 1880s, he invited a young Yankee couple, the Potters, to come dine with him there; when the husband, James, asked what he should wear, the Prince of Wales sent him to his Savile Row tailor, who hooked him up with a tail-less black coat. Wanting to show off to the guys back home how tight he and the future King of England were (never mind the fact that he'd only gotten the invite because the prince had the hots for his wife), Potter took to wearing his precious jacket when he hung out at his country club in Tuxedo Park, a gated getaway for the Knickerbocker elite of Manhattan. Although there are many stories about what happened next, presumably all the club members copied Potter, and when they were out on the town in New York and some dude snarkily asked, "Hey, what the hell is that jacket you Tuxedo guys are wearing?" they got to retort, "Oh, it's what the prince wears—didn't you know?"

For the very first Knickerbocker, see *knickers*.

uto·pia n. *The perfect place, which as such can never exist.*
Utopia is an island five hundred miles in circumference located in the Atlantic Ocean just off the coast of Brazil. Its government is socialist, and there is no private property; although all houses are the same, they are rotated every ten years to make sure nobody feels like they are getting gypped. Similarly, everyone has to wear the exact same outfit. Unemployment stands at zero percent; work is compulsory, but the workday lasts only six hours. There are free hospitals and legalized euthanasia. Divorce is permitted, and advisable for anyone who wants to cheat on their

spouse, as the penalty for adultery is enslavement and, for repeat offenders, death. Religious tolerance is complete and extended to all, except those with no religion. Atheism, though legal, is despised, as those who don't believe in an afterlife are thought to have no stake in right or wrong and are thus considered menaces to society.

This, at least, is what we are told by Thomas More, the title of whose 1516 Latin treatise was originally rendered in English as *A Fruitful and Pleasant Book of the Best State of a Public Weal, and of the New Isle Called Utopia*, nowadays usually shortened to the pithier *Utopia*. More wrote his work at a time when, as he put it, "countries are always being discovered which were not in the old geography books." It is difficult to tell exactly what More admired about his imagined country and what he was ridiculing, but these things happen with satire. In any event, it is ironic that *utopia* has come to mean an ideal place, as More himself clearly disagreed with at least one Utopian custom: legalized divorce. Years after he had written his landmark work and while serving as the King's Lord High Chancellor, the staunchly Catholic More took a principled stand against the dissolution of Henry VIII's marriage, which also dissolved England's official relationship with the church of Rome. More's silent opposition was immortalized in *A Man for All Seasons*, a play that ends—like More's life—with his beheading.

HEAVENS AND HELLS

Few toponyms have enjoyed such rich proverbial use as the places of reward and punishment in the afterlife. A good cupcake is *heavenly*, a bad job *hellish*, and to have to wait for resolution is to be *left in limbo*. *Heaven* and *Hell* were both pagan terms in Old English that got repurposed for Christian use. The Latin term for Hell is *inferno*, popularized by Dante and used mostly in English for a really horrible fire, while *Hades*—used as a euphemism for Hell in the days when such euphemisms were necessary—originates in Greek mythology. A section of Hades was the Elysian Fields, destination for the blessed and heroic. The ancients took these to be quite literal places; the entrance to the underworld, for instance, was placed by the Romans near Lake Avernus. *Eden* makes for a ready metaphor, while *paradise* has become all but completely disconnected from the biblical location. *Paradise* comes to us via Greek, which borrowed the term from an ancient Persian source, where it meant a walled orchard or garden. The Greeks also had Arcadia, a mountain area of the Peloponnesus held to be ideally rustic and representing a life that had otherwise disappeared.

People have never been content to wait for the afterlife to find paradise. Buddhism offers nirvana, not a physical place but a state of mind. The residents of *Shangri-La* live in a permanent state of bliss, but like Utopia the place is fictional, invented by James Hilton for his 1933 novel, *Lost Horizon*, in which a plane makes an emergency landing in the Himalayas and the dying Chinese pilot tells the protagonist he must seek shelter in the monastery of Shangri-La, a mystical place lost out of time whose inhabitants are near immortal, provided they never leave.

A very real place was Xanadu, which nevertheless was so fantastical that its chronicler Marco Polo was believed to be making it up. Children followed him through the streets of Venice mocking him, *Mister Polo, tell us more lies!* and yet most of what he wrote was later corroborated. Xanadu sparked the imagination of such poets as Coleridge, who wrote, "In Xanadu did Kubla Khan/A stately pleasure-dome decree." The dome was really a giant yurt (which is not to downplay the pleasures taking place inside), while Xanadu itself was the great Mongol emperor's retreat from the searing summer heat of his capital in Dadu (modern Beijing). Xanadu was a giant game park stocked with domesticated deer for hunting and two thousand white horses, and is used proverbially as a place of great amusements, as well as for the title of one of the worst movies of all time.

Of all the fabled lost cities of history, the one that has obsessed fortune hunters the most is El Dorado. Francisco Pizarro had already conquered one city of gold—Cuzco, the capital of the Incas—when he began hearing of another, even greater land of gold from the locals, as well as a country of cinnamon, a commodity of similar value. Pizarro sent his little brother Gonzalo to search for it, and the younger conquistador set out east of Quito with about two hundred Spaniards, four thousand natives, and his second in command, Francisco de Orellana, in early 1541. A year later the expedition was in tatters, with three quarters of everyone dead. Gonzalo turned back, but Orellana persevered; while he didn't find El Dorado, Orellana saw a lot of cinnamon trees, and discovered and explored the entire length of a great river that—after having been attacked by a fierce tribe of female warriors—he named the Amazon. As for El Dorado, people have searched for it ever since; Sir Walter Raleigh believed he had found it on a lake in Guyana, while Percy Fawcett died looking for it in the jungles of Mato Grasso, Brazil, in 1925. Percy, however, esoterically called it the Lost City of Z, which in this form has finally conferred riches on someone, having become publishing and movie gold for writer David Grann.

See *Timbuktu* for lands of gold; *serendipity* for lands of cinnamon.

vaude·ville *n. Something your grandparents found amusing.*

Vaudeville had its U.S. heyday from the 1880s through the 1930s, when it was eclipsed by the one-two punch of radio and the movies. But despite its deep, kitschy roots in America, vaudeville's ultimate origins are French, or rather, Norman. The vaux-de-Vire, or valley of the Vire, lies in the Calvados region of Normandy. Nestled in its rocky ravines was once found the mill of a fuller named Olivier Basselin. A fuller cleans and makes wool thicker—i.e., fuller—by a process that has a dreadlocking effect on the fibers. Although the mill paid the bills, Basselin's passion was for song. His music was not the refined sort but of the common man, or at least the common Norman man, who was thought to be a good deal coarser, at least by other Frenchmen. Basselin's songs, written in the first half of the fifteenth century, were about drinking and love and drinking some more. His oeuvre includes such classics as "To My Nose," about the effect the drink had on the color of his proboscis, and "Apology for Cider," which goes like this:

> *Though Frenchmen at our drink may laugh*
> *And think their taste is wondrous fine,*
> *The Norman cider, which we quaff,*
> *Is quite the equal of his wine.*

For more of what the French thought of the Normans, see *bigot*.

6 CATS 9 DOGS 3 HORSES

In nature, you find species; in domesticated animals, you find breeds. Whereas every fox looks more or less the same, dogs have a wider variety of size, shape, and aspect than any other species on the planet. Because breeds are created in isolation—be it a region, town, or farm—they lend themselves to toponymous titling. To present an exhaustive list would be just that: exhausting. So instead, find a curated selection below*:

FELINES

1. *Siamese*: Perhaps the most famous feline breed, the first of these talkative creatures came to the West via the American consul stationed in Siam, who presented it as a gift to President Hayes.

---

*The preponderance of canine breeds should not be taken as preferential treatment; the inclusion of Siamese and Maine coon cats, however, should.

2. *Manx*: An odd cat from an odd place. Although it lies in the Irish Sea, the Isle of Man is not a part of the United Kingdom, and until recently a unique form of Gaelic was spoken by the Manx (the people, not the cats). Due to a genetic defect, the cats native to the island have no tail.

3 & 4. *Cornish rex, Devon rex*: Having no fur—or not very much of it—are the genetic mutations of a couple of English breeds. The occurrences were unique: The first C-Rex was born on a farm in Cornwall in the 1950s, the original D-Rex found in an abandoned tin mine in Devon in the 1960s.

5. *Maine coon*: Not lacking in fur in any way, this cat is one of the oldest American breeds and is indeed from Maine; as for the second part of its name, theories suggest that the breed descended either from a cat belonging to a Captain Coon or from a feline-raccoon mating. (The latter theory perhaps from people who have watched too many Pepé Le Pew cartoons.)

6. *Cheshire cat*: Not a breed but a simile. It was made famous by *Alice in Wonderland*, but to grin like a Cheshire cat was an old saying, meaning to have a gummy or toothy smile, perhaps in reference to a cheese sold in Cheshire, England, that was molded in the shape of a feline grinning from ear to ear.

Canines

1. *Labrador retriever*: From Labrador, one of the maritime provinces of Canada; whether chocolate or yellow, the Lab is by far the most popular breed of dog in America.

2. *Great Dane*: Known as Danish dogs before their promotion in 1749, when the French took to calling the breed *le Grand Danois*; they are largest dog in the world.

3. *Chihuahua*: The smallest breed in the world, this dog was found in 1850 living in the ruins of what may have been an Aztec palace in the state of Chihuahua, Mexico, which led to speculation that it is the descendant of a breed known to have served pre-Columbian religious leaders in rituals dating back to Mayan times.

4. *Lhasa apso*: Another dog with a long-held religious gig is this terrier from the Tibetan capital of Lhasa, a breed that has been sounding the alarm in Buddhist temples since 800 B.C. (which is 17,660 B.C. in dog years).

5. *Airedale*: Known as the "king of terriers" for its unusual height, this descendant of a terrier and an otterhound was bred in the valley of the River Aire in England, and enjoys hunting the occasional otter itself.

6. *Cocker spaniel*: The woodcock is the prey of choice for this dog, hence *cocker*; the *spaniel* part comes from the Old

French *Espaignol*, meaning Spanish, although the connection between the breed and Spain remains unknown.

7. *Pomeranian*: While this toy pooch sits on the lap of heiresses pounding glasses of rosé and Cristal on St. Barths, its cousins are working the Iditarod, as one would expect of dogs descended from Arctic wolves. Named after Pomerania, a Prussian region in what is now Poland.

8. *Rottweiler*: Rottweil, Germany, is an ancient Roman town, and its breed is said to descend from drover dogs that accompanied the Roman legions while on campaign; later, they not only herded livestock but hauled dog carts piled up with meat, which earned them their other name, *Metzgerhund*, which means "butcher dog."

9. *Dalmatian*: Instead of pulling wagons, these dogs from the ex-Venetian coast of Dalmatia had an affinity for following them, which is why they were known as coach dogs. Their origin as firehouse dogs dates to the time of the horse-drawn fire wagon; these days, one accompanies the Budweiser Clydesdales.

EQUINES

1. *Clydesdale*: From the valley of the River Clyde, this shaggy Scottish horse can weigh as much as a ton and be twenty hands tall; this industrial-strength beast of burden

is perfectly suited to pulling heavily laden wagons over rough uneven cobbles and through ditches of mud, or trotting majestically through leafy streets in Super Bowl commercials.

2. *Shetland pony*: Also from Scotland—in this case the Shetland Islands—this breed is like a wee Clydesdale, measuring as little as seven hands but still a working draft horse. This made them the ideal pit ponies, sadly for them, as that meant they were sent to live in underground mines hauling coal, yet further victims of the industrial revolution.

3. *Lippizzaner*: Geographically confusing to say the least, these high-hoofing horses, traditionally bred on a stud farm in Lippizza in modern-day Slovenia, are trained by the Spanish Riding School of Vienna, Austria. (For why they should never be used in battle, see *sybarite*.)

APPENDIX II

TERROIR: A MENU

In an age when all good foodies demand to know precisely where their food comes from, could there be a better time to open a restaurant dedicated to toponymous foodstuffs? Our establishment is called Terroir, originally a French enological term meaning the character a wine derived from its place of origin, a term since extended to food in general.

--WINES--

As befits a restaurant named Terroir, we serve only vins Français, *with a selection from the following regions. (We do keep a straw-covered bottle of Chianti hanging from the rafters, for those sentimental for the Chianti hills around Florence. It is empty.)*

Beaujolais - Bordeaux - Burgundy - Chablis - Champagne

Chablis and Bordeaux are villages, while Beaujolais is named after the hamlet of Beaujeu. Between Beaujeu and Chablis lie the towns of Gamay and Chardonnay (whose grapes are featured in many of our offerings), all of which sit in the state of Burgundy, named after the Burgundians, a Germanic tribe that overran Roman Gaul. Champagne is likewise a French state (or region), from a word meaning "country."

--BRANDIES--

Like our wines, all are from France.

Armagnac - Cognac - Calvados

Armagnac and Cognac are towns in southwestern France, while Calvados is a department of Normandy. (Calvados is made from apples; for more on the hard-drinking Normans' love of hard cider, see *vaudeville.*)

--FORTIFIED WINES--

A particular specialty of our restaurant, and of Iberia.

Madeira - Port - Sherry - Amontillado - Marsala

Fortified wines were popular in Britain and America during the age of sail, when alcohol (often brandy) was added to casks of wine to keep them from spoiling on long ocean voyages. The Madeira Islands were a natural place for such wines to develop, being Portugal's version of the Canary Islands, the jumping-off spot for New World voyages that originated in Oporto, the Portuguese capital and home of port wine. Spanish boats instead left from Cádiz, the port closest to the city of Jerez, corrupted in English to *sherry.* Further inland is the town of Montilla, home of amontillado, a kind of sherry, as well as a lure for a murder victim in Edgar Allan Poe's "The Cask of Amontillado." Lastly comes the wine of Marsala, Sicily, an island that was long a possession of the Spanish, whose influence can be noted in the use of the honorific *Don* (as in Juan, and Corleone).

*All menu items are Market Price.

Bourbon - Tequila - Scotch

Bourbon is a county in Kentucky, Tequila a town in Mexico, and Scotch an impolite term in reference to the Scottish people, but the correct word for their whisky. We feature Glenlivet and Glenfiddich, which come from the narrow valleys—or glens—of the Rivers Livet and Fiddich.

--LIQUEUR--

Curaçao

Curaçao is a country whose namesake liqueur was originally made with the peels of the *laraha*, a citrus fruit descended from Valencia oranges brought to the island in the early 1500s from Spain.

--BEER--

We favor Mitteleuropean brews.

Pilsner - Budweiser - Bock

Bock comes from the German town of Einbock, while our other beers come from Pilsen and Budweis, towns in the Bohemia region of the Czech Republic. Our Budweiser is not the weak lager you buy in cans by the case, but the Old World original. (The *-er* is crossed out because it is illegal in the U.S. to sell the beer under its regular name, due to a territorial agreement with Anheuser-Busch.)

--WATER--

Evian - San Pellegrino

From Évian-les-Bains, France, and San Pellegrino Terme, Italy. Although we make a killing on the imported stuff, the environmentally friendly staff of Terroir would prefer that you order a bottle of our own seltzer. (To make an informed decision, see *seltzer*.)

--CHEESE--

Spain: **Manchego** - Italy: **Asiago, Gorgonzola, Parmigiano** (Parma) - Switzerland: **Emmentaler** (Emmental), **Gruyère** (Gruyères) - France: **Munster, Camembert, Brie, Roquefort** - Netherlands: **Edam, Gouda** - England: **Cheddar, Stilton** - Norway: **Jarlsberg** - USA: **Colby** (Wisconsin), **Monterey Jack** (Monterey, California)

Manchego hails from Don Quixote's home region of La Mancha. Spanish cheesemakers—specifically Franciscan friars—brought their ways to the New World, influencing a California land magnate and dairy owner named David Jack, as in Monterey. (Parmesan, as in the containers of sandy faux-cheese pebbles with a French spelling, is not served here.)

Salade Niçoise - Insalata Caprese - Romaine

The first two are Mediterranean creations, from the city of Nice and the isle of Capri. Romaine comes from the French word for Roman, a lettuce we serve with Thousand Island dressing, created by Oscar of the Waldorf and named in honor of the St. Lawrence River region.

--SOUP--

Vichyssoise

A collaborationist soup honoring Vichy, France, created by a New York hotel legend, Ritz chef Louis Diat.

--ENTREES--

Pheasant - Steak Tartare - Sardines

The ancient Greeks believed pheasants came from the region of the Phasis River in what is present-day Georgia. Steak tartare pays homage to the preferred way of eating beef (raw) by Genghis Khan's horde, a mix of various races of Turks, Cossacks, and Kirghiz Tatars, the last of whose name was altered by Europeans who believed they had come from Tartarus, or Hell. We serve your choice of beef, either Kobe (after the port city in Japan) or Angus (the county in Scotland). Speaking of the Tartars, with the sardines—found plentifully around the island of Sardinia—we serve tartar sauce, so-called for the rough chopping of vegetables. We make ours the traditional way, with mayonnaise, which hails from Port Mahon, Minorca, and Worcestershire sauce, made originally by Messrs. Lea and Perrins in Worcester, England, in the 1830s.

--VEGETABLE SIDES--

Lima Beans - Brussels Sprouts - Portobello Mushrooms - Scallions

Our first two vegetables come from the capitals of Peru and Belgium, respectively, while the name of our mushroom comes from Portobelo, Panama, a port city off which a great battle was waged and won by Admiral Edward "Old Grog" Vernon (for whom a sailor's drink is named). Portobello Road in London ultimately derives its name in honor of that victory, but how it got to be the name of an oversize cremini mushroom is unclear. Scallions, however, we know get their name from being the "onions of Ascalon." This Philistine city (present-day Ashkelon, Israel) is also the source behind *shallot*, via French. (We no longer serve Jerusalem artichoke, as we have learned it is not from Jerusalem at all.)

We specialize in flaky pastries.

Napoleon - Danish

Napoleon here does not refer to a little Corsican, but to the city of Naples (from a corruption of Napolitano or Napolitain). Our danishes are done the traditional way, filled with marzipan, a name that derives from the town of Martaban, Burma.

--COFFEE--

Turkish - French Press - Café Mocha

The word *coffee* has been conjectured to come from Kaffa, the name of a kingdom in the Ethiopian highlands, where the plant is native and still grows wild. On the other side of the Red Sea is the port city of Mocha, Yemen, through which coffee was long exported; *mocha* still refers to beans from there, as well as the drink that is made flavored with chocolate, and a color.

--BAR MENU--

Buffalo Wings - Frankfurter, or Wiener - Hamburger - French Fries

Buffalo wings were first made to satisfy the munchies of bargoers in Buffalo, New York, in the 1960s. With origins stretching farther back are what were originally called the Frankfurter wurst and wienerwurst, the sausages of Frankfurt and Vienna (Wien), respectively. (We serve with Dijon, a mustard named after a French city.) Our hamburger is served on a bialy, a roll that Ashkenazi Jews brought from Bialystok, Poland, to the New World; we recommend American or Swiss cheese and a shot of Tabasco sauce, from the name of a river and state in Mexico. Hamburgers were once called Hamburg Steaks, after the city in Germany, while French fries evolved from French frieds, short for French-fried potatoes. Both underwent wartime renaming, the former called Liberty Steaks during World War I (mostly out of patriotism), and the latter called Freedom Fries at the onset of the Second Gulf War (mostly out of stupidity).

APPENDIX III

ET CETERA

Because you can never quite have enough, here are some toponyms that still seem worth mentioning.

ascot: A knotted neckerchief as worn at the oh-so-fashionable races at Ascot Heath.

bantam: From Bantam, Dutch Java; first an undersized but feisty rooster, then a weight class.

badminton: Assumedly, from Badminton House, an estate in Gloucestershire, but how and why is unknown.

bronze: From medieval Latin *bronzium*, it seems from earlier Latin *Brondusium*—of Brindisi.

bungalow: From Hindi *Bangla*, meaning Bengali, for their style of house: one-story, small, and not too sturdy.

copper: Mined on the island of Cyprus.

cravat: From the soldier-casual style of Croat mercenaries hanging around Paris in the Thirty Years' War.

Ebola virus: The Ebola River, a tributary of the Congo and site of a 1976 epidemic.

Epsom salts: From Epsom, England, site of a hot spring rich in magnesium sulfate, discovered because a farmer's cows refused to drink from it during a drought.

geyser: In the valley of Haukadalur, Iceland, there is a hot spring completely different from the one found at Spa; it is called the Geysir.

italics: First used by Venetian printer Aldus Manutius for a 1501 edition of the *Aeneid*, the epic story of the Italic people; Italics *lean*, Roman doesn't.

jodhpurs: The residents of Jodhpur, India, favored a tight-fitting trouser that British colonialists noticed was excellent to wear in the saddle.

Jurassic: The period comes from the Jura mountain range that straddles France and Switzerland.

limousine: In reference to a hood worn by herders in the Limousin region of France; why it got applied to a car with passenger and chauffeur traveling in separate compartments is unknown.

rugby: A sport whose rules were first drawn up by players at the Rugby School.

sisal: A fiber product made from the agave plant, as sold in Sisal, a port in the Yucatán.

spruce: Whether the evergreen tree or, as a verb, to spiffy something up, this word comes from an old alteration of *Prussia* used in reference to its products.

suede: *Gants de Suede* were the rage in nineteenth-century France; literally kid gloves from Sweden.

tangerine: From Tangier, Morocco.

telemark: You either know what this is, or you don't care. Telemark, Norway.

varnish: The ancient Libyan town of Berenike pioneered the use of varnishes. The way people pronounce things has changed a lot since it did.

AFTERWORD

In putting a book like this together, you live for those moments when you discover an unexpected oddity of word history, such as learning that *coach* comes from the name of a town in Hungary. The downer moments arrive when you realize that a word isn't what it seemed to be. One entry for this book involved Roman conquest, the history of wooden footwear, B. F. Goodrich, the invention of vulcanized rubber, and L.L. Bean, but I had to delete it when I found out that *galoshes* likely doesn't derive from *Gaulish shoes* but *kalopous*, an ancient Greek word for a shoemaker's block.

The older the word, the murkier its etymology. *Gallery* may come from Galilee and *dagger* from Dacia, an ancient Roman name for Romania; a kind of dagger called the *pistolese* originated in the Tuscan town of Pistoia, a center of firearms manufacture that may also have given the world *pistol*.

Guessing at etymologies has long been a literary sport,

popular among no one so much as the ancient Romans. A writer such as Ovid might trot out two or three possible etymologies for the same word just to make a point. An interesting ancient example of toponymity that is hard to verify is *cry*. The Roman writer Varro claimed that imperiled citizens shouting for the Quirites (Roman citizens) was the source behind the Latin verb *quiritare*, which in vulgar Latin became something like *cridar* before settling into the French *crier*. While the OED accepts Varro's explanation as logical, other etymologists consider it folk etymology and say the Latin word is imitative in origin, having had an earlier meaning of "to squeal like a pig."

Any word that represents a sound has at least a decent chance to be onomatopoeic. See the entry *barbarian* for an example of this, or consider the word *mammary*, which comes from the *mama* sound a baby makes when it wants to nurse. But sound enters into the way we acquire words in other equally elemental ways. Note the grouping *bunk/blarney/baloney/bullshit*, or the somewhat puzzling trio of *beggar/bugger/bigot*, the exact development of all three of which are shrouded in the murk of the Middle Ages but all of which meant "heretic" at one point. Unconsciously, our brain puts words that sound alike into the same category of meaning. What a wonderful word is *maelstrom*, with its Germanic-sounding echo of malevolence and storm. *Bikini* was the perfect word for a two-part item, as our mind files it alongside *bivalve* and *bisexual*. And note how massive *arm*ies gathering for *arm*ed conflict leads to *Arm*ageddon.

Yet our brains are just as likely to tempt us into believing urban legends. The most famous one comes from the lobby of the Willard Hotel, where President Ulysses S. Grant was said to enjoy his cigar and brandy but hated being besieged by favor seekers, the people he supposedly called "those damn lobbyists." I was similarly convinced after visiting Chicago that to be "in the loop" must have come from the concentration of business and newspaper titans within the Loop; it didn't. (It is aviation lingo.) While Limousin, France, seems to have some connection to the development of a type of automobile, Sedan, France, almost certainly doesn't, despite claims to the contrary. Other foreign toponyms with no connection to English words include Dildo, Newfoundland, and Fucking, Austria, which can't keep from getting its signs stolen.

Also not included in this book are words that come from people's names that just happen to be toponyms. My last book, *Anonyponymous*, included such examples of this as *maudlin*, a corruption of the epithet Magdalene, as in Mary Magdalene, or Mary of Magdala. There was also the double-toponym name of John Duns Scotus, a Scottish guy named John from the town of Duns, although only his last name figures into the word *dunce*. The toponym-to-surname-to-eponym phenomenon occurs most frequently with the nobility; consider such folks as the Marquis de Sade, the Lords Derby and Cardigan, and John Montagu, the Fourth Earl of Sandwich.

In closing, it is worth noting that the way toponyms enter our language has been changing. Previously, words coming from the name of a people tended to be disparaging, especially if their homelands were found in the British Isles and not named England. While we've done a lot recently to scrub English clean, some of these slanders are hidden in the language in plain sight, e.g., *paddy wagon*. Toponyms are also being legally restricted from entering the language, as countries and municipalities use the courts to enforce place-name trademarks on their products. The EU seems largely to exist to adjudicate such matters, and any potential conflicts must be cleared up before a country can join that family of nations, as was the case with the squabble over the Venetian wine called Tocai, named after a grape, and the Hungarian wine Tokaji, named after a place called Tokaj. (Hungary won.) And even the most time-honored way of place names entering English has been turned on its head. No longer would the porter of Baghdad be so impressed by the shopping choices of the lady with the Mosul cloak. Now, far from distance conferring prestige on a product, consumers go to great lengths to buy fruits and vegetables grown as close to their homes as possible.

The distance between Us and Them is getting shorter.

NOTES

10 (in 1782, to be exact): "Ammonia" was coined in 1782 by Swedish chemist Torbern Bergman from *sal ammoniac*, now known as ammonium chloride.

14 a mangling of the Arabic term *hashishiyyin*, meaning "user of hashih": Users, actually, as *-in* is a plural suffix in Arabic. A similar ending exists in Hebrew, which English preserves in the plural of *cherub*, *cherubim*.

17 by Basque hunters in Bayonne: According to the Oxford English Dictionary, other etymologies for *bayonet* have been suggested, including links to the Old French *bayon* or *baion* ("arrow or shaft of a crossbow"), the Spanish *bayona* ("sheath"), and the Italian *bajonetta* ("little joker," a *Scarface*-esque nickname for a dagger).

18 any dude who wanted to call himself a Beguin: *Beguin* is the masculine form of *Beguine*.

18 a word that obviously needed inventing: *To beg* seems to come from French *beguiner*, "to act the beguin," while *beggar* perhaps comes directly from *Beghard*.

18 the world's first phonetic . . . writing system: The Phoenicians were building on an earlier system begun by fellow Canaanites who are thought to have been guest workers in Egypt.

23 *Scotch*: To scotch something, as in to put a stop to it, sounds like a slur but is actually from the archaic verb *scocchen*. *Hopscotch*, no slur at all, is from yet another root.

26 $150 million: Despite the reparations fund, some of the Bikini Atollers are still battling the U.S. government in court to settle their claims.

31 Albigensians were ascetics: Technically, it was only the Perfect who were true ascetics; the followers didn't tread so narrow a path, only becoming Perfect on their deathbed.

32 "I shall not be speaking to the House, but to Buncombe": Others record that Walker said that he was "bound to do some talkin' for Buncombe," or "must make a speech for the Buncombe papers."

36 a gaggle of nymphs: In other traditions, the minders were a pair of sisters; see the story of Hercules' eleventh labor, p. 65.

36 mostly about lizards and a few ruined buildings: At least that was the account according to the great Roman naturalist Pliny, our secondhand source for the accounts of Juba's expedition.

50   Giovanni Farina first manufactured his scent in 1709: The credit for who first concocted eau de Cologne is a dispute spilling across centuries. In 1907 a German court ruled that the inventor was Giovanni Feminis, another immigrant from Val Vigezzo.

50   naming it after his adopted town: Actually, the French version of the name of his adopted town. Cologne's German name, Köln, probably wouldn't have had the same impact. In either case the name comes from the same source, the Latin word *colonia*, meaning simply "colony."

50   *toilet water*: A literal translation of *eau de toilette*, the English phrase suffered after *toilet* went from meaning "dressing room" to "bathroom" to the porcelain apparatus therein, a victim of the euphemism treadmill.

51   People living in high elevations: The problem was not limited to the Alps, but found around the world in mountainous areas with limestone terrain. Note ancient scroll images from the East that depict mountain people suffering from goiters.

52   *This Side of Paradise*: Besides *daiquiri*, the novel also contains the first known citation of *T-shirt*.

56   *va fa in culo*: The phrase essentially means "go fuck yourself in the ass."

58   took to indiscriminately calling . . . all Christians—Franks: Or rather *Faranji*, an Arabic word that spread to India as *Feringhees*, where it became deeply pejorative.

58   it simply meant "free": The association of *frank* with freedom is present in a word that English adopted from Norman French, *franchise*, meaning the right to vote, though the term has evolved to the point where it now means the right to serve disgusting food as well, among other things.

59   the Phrygian cap: In ancient imagery depicting the Trojan War, the fighters on the Trojan side are often distinguished by their Phrygian caps, while King Midas is usually shown sporting one to hide his donkey ears, given to him by Apollo after Midas told the god he wasn't so great at playing the lyre.

64   hunter-gatherer peoples also called Pygmies: *Pygmy* has become a politically incorrect term for these tribes, although the name, much like with Gypsy, stubbornly sticks, mostly because no other umbrella term for them exists, and no one would know who you were talking about if you mentioned the Bayaka or Bambenga. Also, they don't have a real strong lobby.

67   prefer the term *Roma* or *Romany*: These terms have nothing to do with the group's heavy concentration in Romania, but rather come from the Gypsy word *rom*, meaning "man."

67   why did they leave India: The real reason the Romany left India may never be known, but many theories argue for a military connection of some kind. More prosaically, the group may have been fleeing persecution, not for the last time.

68   a Canterbury, or canter: Originally, a Canterbury pace, trot, or gallop.

70   Tyrian purple: The dye was so precious, and its association with royalty so strong, that in Byzantium royals were not "blue bloods" but "born in the purple." In Ancient Rome, the dye was reserved for use by the emperor, top officials, and military commanders; Nero was an especially big fan.

75   *Sleasie*, or *sleazy*: The connection is disputed: In the late seventeenth century there are references both to *Sleasie cloth* from Silesia and to *sleasie* as describing fabric that was poorly made. The OED calls the connection unlikely, but it seems hard to believe that there is no link whatsoever.

77   *Gotham*: Literally *got-ham*, short for "goat hamlet," after a fictional town of idiots in England.

82   the Laconic reply: Other sources have the Macedonian saying, "If I win this war, you will be slaves forever." Whatever his message, Philip and his son Alexander the Great avoided Sparta after that. (The story, incidentally, is not the source of the term, but the most oft-cited example of Laconic brevity.)

83   *Mother of beauty, mother of joy*: Bliss Carman, *Sappho: One Hundred Lyrics* (Boston: L.C. Page and Company, 1904), 16.

85   The filthy version: "There was an old man from Nantucket/Whose dick was so long he could suck it./Said he with a grin/As he wiped off his chin/If my ear were a cunt I could fuck it."

86   how did *lumber* get to mean "wood"?: The verb *lumber*, meaning "to walk clumsily," is also brought up as a possible source, although the connection is unclear.

87   *strom*, stream, with *maalen*, to mill or grind: The words are Dutch.

90   called by the Greeks *Magnes lithos*, "Magnesian stone": Pliny, however, attributes the word to "the name of a shepherd, Magnes, who found that the ground on Mount Ida attracted the iron nails in his shoes and

the ferrule of his staff." Magnesia is also ultimately behind the names for the elements manganese (symbol Mn, atomic number 25) and magnesium (Mg, number 12). Milk of Magnesia, incidentally, is a proprietary name for the suspension of magnesium hydroxide in water.

91   twenty-two miles: Herodotus tells a different tale, having the world's first marathon runner go from Athens to Sparta, a distance of 150 miles.

92   A remarkable array of Indian titles: Going farther east, *tycoon* comes from Japanese *taikun*, while the term *Grand Poobah* is derived from the Gilbert and Sullivan operetta *The Mikado*, set in Japan; the character Pooh-Bah was the "Lord High Everything Else," spoofing English interest in the titles of the exotic East. The additional title of "Grand," incidentally, was an innovation from *The Flintstones*, the Grand Poobah being the pinnacle of power in the Loyal Order of Water Buffaloes.

94   Mongoloids: Mongolian was one of Johann Blumenbach's five races of humanity. He seems to have adopted the term from another, more racist German, Christoph Meiners, who believed that there were only two races: Caucasian and Mongolian—i.e., whites and everyone else. Like Caucasoid and Negroid, the form Mongoloid became popular among proponents of racial theories because words ending in *-oid* sounded scientific.

96   pall-mall: From *pallamaglio*, "ball mallet" in Italian.

98   "the One Who Warns": This epithet owes to some sacred geese from Juno's temple waking up Rome when the city was being surreptitiously invaded by Gauls. At least this was the popular etymology in ancient days; it is now disputed.

100   Neanderthal–homo sapien hanky-panky: According to research published in 2010, between 1 and 4 percent of the DNA sequence of modern, non-African humans is inherited from Neanderthals, a relatively small amount. Genome comparison places the interbreeding as having taken place 45,000 to 85,000 years ago; but since the Neanderthals didn't disappear from the fossil record until 30,000 years ago, it is unlikely they were absorbed and assimilated out of existence.

105   Bohemian folk dance: The name *polka* is said to be a commemoration of the November Uprising of the Poles against Russia in the 1830s.

105   The Schottische . . . the Watusi: *Schottische* is German for Scottish; the Watusi are now more commonly known as the Tutsi.

109   Horace Walpole: Walpole's most enduring legacy has to do with the gothic. He pioneered and coined the literary genre with his work *The*

Castle of Otranto, which in its second edition was subtitled *A Gothic Story*, and is also credited with creating the neo-Gothic architectural trend with his house Strawberry Hill. *Gothic* in regard to the arts originally meant "not classical," specifically pre-Renaissance architecture, and was pejorative; the term was rehabilitated in the Romantic period and found another use at the end of the punk movement, when Siouxsie (of the Banshees) is said to have coined the term *goth* in reference to a style of fashion and music.

110   from a handprint (don't ask) and a good sniff of urine . . . (really don't ask): But if you *must* ask, the urine led one of the princes to deduce that the rider of the camel was a woman because the smell of it turned him on; the handprint showed that she was pregnant because she had to help herself up.

111   The Cinnamon bird: Aristotle bought the story hook, line, and sinker, but Pliny was not so gullible; he thought merchants had invented the story to drive up the price of the spice.

118   The Silk Road: *Silk Road* is the translation of a nineteenth-century German term and a bit of a misnomer, as there was not a single Silk Road but many.

120   Greek word *sklabos*: The term also entered Arabic as *saqaliba*, the market for Slavs being especially vigorous in Al-Andalus, the Emirate of Sicily, and North Africa. Closer to what Slavs called themselves is *Slovene*, a word believed to come from an Old Slav root meaning "to speak." In English, *slave* replaced *thrall*; note that the verb *enthrall* once meant "to enslave."

125   pillar of salt: Today in Israel you can find a craggy outcropping on Mount Sodom called Lot's Wife. It, like the rest of Mount Sodom, is made of rock salt.

136   A condom: Trojan condoms were first sold by Young's Rubber in 1920, and trademarked in 1927. With an overwhelming share of the U.S. market, *trojan* came to mean a condom in general.

138   all this stuff back from India: The idea that the conquistadors were bringing the birds back from India was widespread, as evidenced by the French *coq d'inde* (Indian cock); in Turkey itself, the bird is called a *hindi*.

138   his country estate at Cowes: A tuxedo coat was also called a "Cowes coat" and is known in England as a dinner jacket (which, confusingly, refers to a white tuxedo coat in America). In continental Europe the outfit is known by the English word *smoking*, as seen in German *der smoking* and Italian *lo smoking* (which really confuses things, as in

English a smoking jacket is one made of velvet or brocade).

140 is ironic that *utopia* has come to mean an ideal place: *Utopia* itself literally means "not a place" in Greek.

144 valley of the Vire: Though most etymologist trace *vaudeville* back to *chanson du Vau de Vire*, "song of the valley of the Vire," some note another popular musical form in the sixteenth century known as "voix de ville" ("town voices").

144 "To My Nose": Selected lyrics include, "The glass [is] my pencil for thine illumination,/My color is the wine/With which I've painted you more red than the carnation."

146 *Maine coon*: Others think the original Maine coons were Marie Antoinette's Turkish angora cats; or that they descended from cats the Vikings brought to the Americas in the eleventh century.

153 Jerusalem artichoke . . . not from Jerusalem: Also not an artichoke. Rather, it is the root of a kind of sunflower, the Italian word for which, *girasole*, got confused with the Holy Land city. This is an example of folk etymology. Another is the English horn, which could more accurately be called a Silesian oboe. The German name for the instrument was *engellisches* horn, which was heard as either "angel's horn" (as intended) or "English horn" (as misunderstood). This was translated as *cor anglais* into French, and from French into English.

INDEX